The View from Jacob's Ladder

ONE HUNDRED MIDRASHIM

The View
from Jacob's Ladder
ONE HUNDRED MIDRASHIM

David Curzon

The Jewish Publication Society
Philadelphia and Jerusalem

Manufactured in the United States of America

The Library of Congress Cataloging-in-Publication Data
Curzon, David.
    The view from Jacob's ladder : one hundred midrashim / David
Curzon.
        p.   cm.
Includes index.
ISBN 0–8276–0568–4
1. Bible.   O.T.–Commentaries.   2. Bible.   O.T.–Meditations.
I. Title.
BS1151.2.C67   1996
221.6–dc20   96–31931
                                    CIP
Designed by Arlene Putterman
Typeset in Palatino by Bill Frambes Typesetting

In memory of Lillian Curzon
and Maurice Curzon (Czerchowski)
and of the family
who remained in Poland
and were murdered

Contents

Acknowledgments

I am grateful to Ellen Frankel, Editor-in-Chief of The Jewish Publication Society, whose enthusiasm for my prose midrashim was the origin of this book; Stanley H. Barkan, who published my first collection of midrashic poems, which became the origin of several subsequent books; Jeffrey Fiskin, who read all drafts and, through his comments and suggestions, helped write most of the pieces collected here; Sharon Friedman, who guided and represented me in the world of publishing; members of Minyan M'at, who heard the sets of interpretations, and some of the individual prose midrashim, as drashes on the portion of the week, and so provided both the occasion that gave rise to them and the audience for which they were first intended; and to Deborah Brodie, Bert Gross and Kusum Singh, Itzhak and Doron Galnoor, Gershom Gorenberg, Ya'acov Hanoch, Burt Visotzky, Gail and Zellman Warhaft, and others who encouraged me.

The author gratefully acknowledges the following publications where some of these poems and prose pieces have appeared:

Midrashim, Chapbook No. 5, Jewish Writers Series,
   Cross-Cultural Communications, 1991
Sewanee Review
Central Park
Tikkun
Forward
Confrontation
Kerim
The Melton Journal
Westerly (Australia)
Tel Aviv Review (Israel)
Helikon (Israel; in Hebrew translation)
HaDoah (in Hebrew translation)
The Jerusalem Report (Israel)

The Jewish Quarterly (United Kingdom)

Some of the poems in this book have been reproduced in the following anthologies:

Chapters into Verse: Poetry in English Inspired by the Bible, Oxford University Press, New York, 1993.

Modern Poems on the Bible: An Anthology, The Jewish Publication Society of America, 1994.

The Oxford Book of Australian Religious Verse, Oxford University Press (Aust.), 1994.

The Tikkun Anthology, Tikkun Books, 1992.

Grateful acknowledgment is made to the following for permission to reprint material:

The parable on page 51 from *Parables and Paradoxes* by Franz Kafka. Copyright © 1946, 1947, 1948, 1953, 1954, 1958 by Schocken Books, Inc. Copyright © renewed 1975 by Schocken Books, Inc. Reprinted by permission of Schocken Books, published by Pantheon Books, a division of Random House, Inc.

Excerpts from *The Koran Interpreted*, by A. J. Arberry, translator, reprinted with permission of Simon and Schuster, Inc., and HarperCollins Publishers Limited. Copyright © 1955 by George Allen and Unwin, Inc.

Isaiah 3:18-23 and 4:4, Psalm 1, Psalm 102:5-8, Psalm 119:1-9, Proverbs 17:1 and Job 2:3-9 and 3:103 from the Revised Standard Version of the Bible, copyright © 1946, 1952, 1971 by the Division of Christian Education of the National Council of the Churches of Christ in the USA. Used by permission.

The two excerpts from Pirke Avot are from Jacob Neusner, *Torah from Our Sages* (Rossel Books, Dallas, 1984), page 74. Reprinted by permission.

The excerpt from the Bet haMidrash is from Raphael Patai, *Gates to the Old City*, Wayne State University Press, Detroit, 1981, reprinted by permission of Raphael Patai.

Preface

Twenty-five years ago I was in an ashram on the banks of the Ganges; ten years later, in New York, after a great deal of meditation, I came to understand that, profound and attractive as Indian religions and philosophies were, I was, in fact, not Hindu.

But I was my psychological self and dreamed my own dreams and made a mess of life in my own way and became preoccupied with all this until, after a great deal of analysis, and another ten years, I came to understand that the self was circumscribed.

I needed some way of discovering my experiences, and moving beyond them, not directly based on my own life. Could it be that the religious texts of my childhood might provide a source of inspiration and a broad common ground with others? After twenty years of avoidance, I gradually and reluctantly started studying the Bible and its commentaries by trying to write poems based on my reading.

The first strategy I adopted was to reject all that could not be immediately read as parables by nonbelievers such as myself. I did not want to violate my sense of integrity and this required, so I thought, not writing any sentence which implied my belief in things beyond the truths of my secular understanding of the world. With the aid of this strategy I reduced 3,000 years and 100,000 pages of erudition, imagination, and wisdom to nothing.

I then decided to preserve my integrity by the opposite strategy of searching for stories and commentaries that were so at variance with secular understanding that no one could ever mistakenly assume I believed in them. For example, Exodus 19:17 tells us that

> Moses brought forth the people out of the camp to meet with God; and they stood at the nether part of the mount.

The King James translation I am quoting here has found a brilliant solution to a peculiarity in the Hebrew. All recent translations have the people standing, sensibly enough, at the "foot" or "base" of Mount Sinai. But the Hebrew has them standing "b'tachteet" of the mountain. This could mean "at the nether world" as well as "at the lower part." The rabbis, of course, noticed this ambiguity and came up with an explanation in the form of a hitherto unknown incident. The *Soncino Chumash* has Rashi attributing the story to "tradition." It appears (in more than one place) in the Talmud; Avodah Zarah 2b recounts it as follows:

> In commenting on the verse: "And they stood at the nether part of the mountain" R. Dimi b. Hama said: This teaches us that the Holy One, blessed be He, suspended the mountain over Israel like a vault [lit., 'cask,' 'tub'] and said to them: 'If you accept the Torah, it will be well with you; if not, here will be your grave.'

When I came across this passage while rummaging in the Talmud I thought to myself, How wonderful; this is my sort of madness. And so:

The Talmud on Free Will

When Moses brought the people from their camp
toward Mount Sinai, where they'd meet with God,
they stood (I quote) "at the nether part of the mount."
But why this strange locution, "nether part"?
It is, says Rabbi Dimi (the son of Hama,
the Babylonian sage), to teach us that
the Holy One lifted the mountain up
(like a huge tub) and held it over them
so all were under the vastness of its base
which blotted out the sun and was, when they
looked up, the only thing they saw. . . .

And so on; the full poem is on page 149. Although this approach yielded several poems, it also reduced the thick riches of the Midrash and the Talmud to a few stories peripheral to the tradition and to my own emerging, ambivalent desire for an engagement with it.

My next strategy was to look at the imaginative devices poets had used to appropriate the biblical texts that inspired them. I made up an anthology of twentieth-century poems based on biblical passages and discovered a whole world of continuity with tradition which required (and this is also traditional) the originality needed to respond to the Book of Job, Adam's Curse, or Lot's Wife with a contemporary sensibility. For example, the Israeli poet Dan Pagis has a poem based on Proverbs 6:6. The well-known text is:

> Go to the ant, thou sluggard; Consider her ways, and be wise.

Pagis, using a midrashic technique, started his poem with the first Biblical line, inserted his response to it, and ended up with a variant on the second Biblical line, namely the more disturbing injunction, implicit in the original, "consider your ways." (Pagis wisely dropped the injunction to "be wise.") I thought to myself, Let me try that, and produced a midrash of my own:

> The Ant
> Proverbs 6:6
>
> *Go to the ant, you sluggard,*
>
> and watch it lug an object
> forward single file
> with no short breaks for
> coffee, gossip, a croissant . . .

The full poem is on page 133. I was beginning to learn the freedom and pleasures of my tradition.

Some texts, however, produced outrage. For example, the first Psalm seemed to me to be an absurd avoidance of the problem posed by the triumph of evil:

> Blessed is the man who walks not in the counsel of the wicked, nor stands in the way of sinners, nor sits in the seat of scoffers . . . The wicked are not so, but are like the chaff which the wind drives away . . . for the LORD knows the way of the righteous, but the way of the wicked will perish.

I was reminded of God's provocation of Cain, as reported in Genesis 4:3-5:

> In the course of time Cain brought to the LORD an offering of the fruit of the ground, and Abel, brought of the firstlings of his flock and of their fat portions. And the LORD had regard for Abel and his offering, But for Cain and his offering he had no regard. So Cain was very angry, and his countenance fell.

This material and my own family history combined to produce a serious poem in a midrashic mode, the full text of which is on page 115:

Psalm 1

Blessed is the man not born
in Lodz in the wrong decade,
who walks not in tree-lined shade
like my father's father in this photo, *nor*
stands in the way of sinners waiting for
his yellow star,
nor sits, if he could sit, in their cattle car . . .

The poem by Dan Pagis was the key; and through the door of my own resistance that it opened, I came to the vast traditions I had been so wary of approaching. I was delighted to learn that these traditions had their own literary devices, and tried using these devices, and found they gave me the freedom to play with the text, to be outraged by the text, to be brought to tears by the text, to be surprised by the strength and nature of my responses, and to begin to discover, through these surprises, myself in my tradition.

A NOTE ON THE BIBLICAL PASSAGES

The passages reproduced are the shortest that include all biblical references in the midrashic responses placed opposite them and whatever additional material seemed needed. My aim was to make the book as self-contained as possible.

Both the Jewish and Christian religious traditions consider the Hebrew Bible a sacred text. In the Jewish tradition it is known as the Tanakh, an acronym based on the Hebrew words for its three divisions, the Torah, the Prophets, and the Writings. In the Christian tradition, it is known as the Old Testament, since it is considered completed by a New Testament. Apart from the names, however, the texts are almost but not quite the same. Of several textual differences between these traditions only two need to be noted here. First, the sequence of books is different. Someone familiar with the Old Testament will be surprised to find in the Tanakh that Psalms, Job, Ecclesiastes, and the other Writings come after the Prophets and not before them. Second, the numbering of the verses in each psalm is different; the Tanakh numbers the headings, while the Old Testament does not. As a result the verse numbers of psalms in the Old Testament are normally one less than those of the corresponding verses in the Tanakh. Verse numbers in some other passages also differ, normally by only plus or minus one.

There are many English translations of the Hebrew Bible available. The norm in this book is whatever translation inspired the midrash opposite. With few exceptions, this is either the 1917 or the 1985 translations of the Jewish Publication Society, which of course follow the Jewish tradition in the sequence of books and the numbering of the psalms. However, if a midrashic response utilizes phraseology from another translation, then that is the one quoted opposite the poem; all translations other than JPS 1917 are cited.

THE MIDRASHIM

The Bible is a mixture of poetry and prose, and the midrashim in this book are a mixture of poetry and prose. Couldn't they all be in prose? No; and for the same reason that Noah's ark had to be made of gopher wood, as explained on page 21.

"Climbing Jacob's Ladder" (pages 46 to 52) is a series of interpretations of Jacob's dream using the rabbinic technique of quoting a "verse from afar" that has no apparent relation to the text, and then showing its application. In this set of midrashim, and in quite a few others, I have used for my verses from afar not only Jewish canonical material but also secular poems and the scriptures of other religions. I hope I have demonstrated in these sections that, with interpretative twists of the sort found in the Midrash, such disparate material can be assimilated to rabbinic modes of discourse. A charming argument for doing so is to be found in Proverbs 31:14:

> She is like the merchant ships;
> She bringeth her food from afar.

If "she" is the Torah, as the Midrash understands, then "her food" is the raw material to be used in interpretation, which must be brought from wherever it exists.

The View
from Jacob's Ladder

ONE HUNDRED MIDRASHIM

A❧ The Creation

Genesis 1:1-5

In the beginning God created the heaven and the earth. [2]Now the earth was unformed and void, and darkness was upon the face of the deep; and the spirit of God hovered over the face of the waters. [3]And God said: 'Let there be light.' And there was light. [4]And God saw the light, that it was good; and God divided the light from the darkness. [5]And God called the light Day, and the darkness He called Night. And there was evening and there was morning, one day.❧

In the Beginning
for Ya'akov Hanoch

In the beginning I was in heaven
to judge from this photo: the plump baby,
on the evidence inside the frame,
even before the first year elapsed,
had established a well-fed character with

no darkness on the face of the deep
and a posture so confident, a look so
knowing—nothing formless or void
in that look!—I'm forced to conclude
there was a time when I'd seen the light.

Soon enough, of course, some sort of darkness
divided from light, and a hesitant spirit
hovered on the face, and there was morning
and now it's afternoon already: one life.

Genesis 1:9-13

⁹And God said: 'Let the waters under the heaven be gathered together unto one place, and let the dry land appear.' And it was so. ¹⁰And God called the dry land Earth, and the gathering together of the waters called He Seas; and God saw that it was good. ¹¹And God said: 'Let the earth put forth grass, herb yielding seed, and fruit-tree bearing fruit after its kind, wherein is the seed thereof, upon the earth.' And it was so. ¹²And the earth brought forth grass, herb yielding seed after its kind, and tree bearing fruit, wherein is the seed thereof, after its kind; and God saw that it was good. ¹³And there was evening and there was morning, a third day.✎

Light

After creating light on the first day, God realized the earth was without form, and void. It was only then that the idea of filling this void occurred to God. And it was only several days later, after creating land, and grasses, and fruit trees, that God arrived at the extraordinary conception of creatures who could see with the aid of light.

B❧ The Garden of Eden

Genesis 2:15-17

¹⁵And the LORD God took the man, and put him into the garden of Eden to dress it and to keep it. ¹⁶And the LORD God commanded the man, saying: 'Of every tree of the garden thou mayest freely eat; ¹⁷but of the tree of the knowledge of good and evil, thou shalt not eat of it; for in the day that thou eatest thereof thou shalt surely die.'❧

Breaking In

The fruit of the Tree of the Knowledge of Good and Evil wasn't an "apple" which is, of course, a mistranslation. And it is a very misleading mistranslation since (it can now be revealed) the real fruit was a pomegranate, which requires its inedible skin to be broken before the edible interior can be reached. It was this act of breaking into the fruit that constituted the sin. Had the fruit been an apple, which can be eaten impulsively skin and all without any prior deliberative act, God would not have been so offended.

Genesis 3:1-5

Now the serpent was more subtle than any beast of the field which the LORD God had made. And he said unto the woman: 'Yea, hath God said: Ye shall not eat of any tree of the garden?' ²And the woman said unto the serpent: 'Of the fruit of the trees of the garden we may eat; ³but of the fruit of the tree which is in the midst of the garden, God hath said: Ye shall not eat of it, neither shall ye touch it, lest ye die.' ⁴And the serpent said unto the woman: 'Ye shall not surely die; ⁵for God doth know that in the day ye eat thereof, then your eyes shall be opened, and ye shall be as God, knowing good and evil.'

The Creatures

The serpent, like all other creatures in the Garden of Eden, had not been forbidden to eat from the Tree of Knowledge. That's why he opened their conversation by asking Eve if any fruit was prohibited. When she told him, he responded with speculations. God was furious, but did not expel the serpent from the Garden because he hadn't actually been disobedient. None of the creatures had eaten the forbidden fruit, and so, being ignorant of good and evil, they remain in Paradise.

Genesis 3:6-7

[6]And when the woman saw that the tree was good for food, and that it was a delight to the eyes, and that the tree was to be desired to make one wise, she took of the fruit thereof, and did eat; and she gave also unto her husband with her, and he did eat. [7]And the eyes of them both were opened, and they knew that they were naked; and they sewed fig-leaves together, and made themselves girdles. ✎

Enticement

When was the first time you reached out and plucked fruit from the tree of the knowledge of good and evil? Think back to childhood. Can you recall an incident which comes close in structure to the biblical account of this emblematic moment we all must experience early in life? No? But we can all have putative memories.

It was like this. There was a neighbor's apple tree that grew to the point where one of its branches hung over our back fence. Let's call the poetic memory "A Neighbor's Apple Tree."

A Neighbor's Apple Tree

The green skin
issued a warning
that I ignored;
I twisted and tore
simple pilfer.

In solitude
I bit into
forbidden fruit;
my tongue shrank
from tart flesh.

Better to gather
only what falls
of its own weight
and the ripeness of
letting go!

Yes; but memory
also embraces
the child's enticement
and his first bite
into bitterness.

C. *The Expulsion*

Genesis 3:22-24

²²And the Lord God said: 'Behold, the man is become as one of us, to know good and evil; and now, lest he put forth his hand, and take also of the tree of life, and eat, and live for ever.' ²³Therefore the Lord God sent him forth from the garden of Eden, to till the ground from whence he was taken. ²⁴So He drove out the man; and He placed at the east of the garden of Eden the cherubim, and the flaming sword which turned every way, to keep the way to the tree of life.

Confession of Faith

Yes, I believe
we are no longer
residing in paradise.

Yes, I believe
there is always a first
murder, and a first
victim, and a third
party whose whispers
could have been resisted.

Yes, I believe
it would have been better
to have never eaten
knowledge of evil.

Yes, I believe
history contains
a flood drowning
almost all.

Yes, the decision
not to permit
our kind to acquire
eternal life
has, I believe,
gained vindication.

D✍ Cain and Abel and After

Genesis 4:1-7

Now the man knew* his wife Eve, and she conceived and bore
Cain, saying, "I have gained† a male child with the help of the LORD."
²She then bore his brother Abel. Abel became a keeper of sheep, and
Cain became a tiller of the soil. ³In the course of time, Cain brought an
offering to the LORD from the fruit of the soil; ⁴and Abel, for his part,
brought the choicest of the firstlings of his flock. The LORD paid heed
to Abel and his offering, ⁵but to Cain and his offering He paid no heed.
Cain was much distressed and his face fell. ⁶And the LORD said to
Cain,✍

> "Why are you distressed,
> And why is your face fallen?
> ⁷‡Surely, if you do right,
> There is uplift.
> But if you do not do right
> Sin couches at the door;
> Its urge is toward you,
> Yet you can be its master."

Translation: JPS 1985

---

* Heb. yada often in the sense of "experienced"
† Heb. qanithi, connected with "Cain"
‡ Heb. verse obscure

Injustice

When Cain's offering was ignored and his face fell, God explained to Cain that he had the capacity to control his natural rage if he wished. But had Cain done so, and calmly and rationally protested the injustice he had suffered, instead of brooding on it, his sacrifice still would not have been accepted since, as God tried to explain, resistance to sin is an end in itself.

Genesis 4:8-16

⁸Cain said to his brother Abel* . . . and when they were in the field, Cain set upon his brother Abel and killed him.

⁹The LORD said to Cain, "Where is your brother Abel?" And he said, "I do not know. Am I my brother's keeper?" ¹⁰Then He said, "What have you done? Hark, your brother's blood cries out to Me from the ground! ¹¹Therefore, you shall be more cursed than the ground, which opened its mouth to receive your brother's blood from your hand. ¹²If you till the soil, it shall no longer yield its strength to you. You shall become a ceaseless wanderer on earth."

¹³Cain said to the LORD, "My punishment is too great to bear! ¹⁴Since you have banished me this day from the soil, and I must avoid Your presence and become a restless wanderer on earth—anyone who meets me may kill me!" ¹⁵The LORD said to him, "I promise, if anyone kills Cain, sevenfold vengeance shall be taken on him." And the LORD put a mark on Cain, lest anyone who met him should kill him. ¹⁶Cain left the presence of the LORD and settled in the land of Nod, east of Eden.➥

Translation: JPS 1985

---

* Ancient versions, including the Targum, read "Come, let us go out into the field."

D. Cain and Abel and After

Rage

Cain tried to control his rage but, as Buddha pointed out some time later, it takes practice to develop skill in self-control, and Cain was given no opportunity to acquire the skill. This is the reason God eventually agreed to mitigate Cain's punishment.

Genesis 5:5

⁵And all the days that Adam lived were nine hundred and thirty years; and he died.🖝

The Facts

After he was expelled from the Garden of Eden, Adam lived to the ripe age of 930. In his last years he reminisced a great deal about the early days, and had rueful thoughts about the way his life had turned out, after such a promising beginning.

But he also had happy memories of his salad days in the Garden. Some of these memories were a little vague, and others a little too lucid. But his pleasant memories, both the vague and the lucid, were of comfort to him. So much is certain from the application of our own experience to the facts as we know them.

E❧ *The Ark*

Genesis 6:11-14

[11]The earth became corrupt before God; the earth was filled with lawlessness. [12]When God saw how corrupt the earth was, for all flesh had corrupted its ways on earth, [13]God said to Noah, "I have decided to put an end to all flesh, for the earth is filled with lawlessness because of them: I am about to destroy them with the earth. [14]Make yourself an ark of gopher wood; make it an ark with compartments, and cover it inside and out with pitch.❧

Translation: JPS 1985

Materials

Why was God so precise in his instructions on building the Ark? Why "gopher" wood? Surely teak or mahogany could have done the job? But those skilled at their craft know the importance of the exact materials. If an inspiration is to take the form of a poem, it could not have been properly realized as prose. Had there been no gopher wood available, there would have been no Ark.

Genesis 8:8-12

[8]And he sent forth a dove from him, to see if the waters were abated from off the face of the ground. [9]But the dove found no rest for the sole of her foot, and she returned unto him to the ark, for the waters were on the face of the whole earth; and he put forth his hand, and took her, and brought her in unto him into the ark. [10]And he stayed yet other seven days; and again he sent forth the dove out of the ark. [11]And the dove came in to him at eventide; and lo in her mouth an olive-leaf freshly plucked; so Noah knew that the waters were abated from off the earth. [12]And he stayed yet other seven days; and sent forth the dove; and she returned not again unto him any more.

Yearning

The second time Noah sent out the dove it found an olive tree, where it rested before returning with a leaf. The third time, we are told, the dove did not return. Why not? Because all sentient beings have the power of choice. Had the dove felt a yearning to return, it would have done so.

F⁊ The Tower of Babel

Genesis 11:1-9

All the earth had the same language and the same words. ²And as men migrated from the east, they came upon a valley in the land of Shinar and settled there. ³They said to one another, "Come, let us make bricks and burn them hard."—Brick served them as stone, and bitumen served them as mortar.—⁴And they said, "Come, let us build us a city, and a tower with its top in the sky, to make a name for ourselves; else we shall be scattered all over the world." ⁵The LORD came down to look at the city and tower which man had built, ⁶and the LORD said, "If, as one people with one language for all, this is how they have begun to act, then nothing that they may propose to do will be out of their reach. ⁷Let us, then, go down and confound their speech there, so that they shall not understand one another's speech." ⁸Thus the LORD scattered them from there over the face of the whole earth; and they stopped building the city. ⁹That is why it was called Babel,* because there the LORD confounded† the speech of the whole earth; and from there the LORD scattered them over the face of the whole earth.⁊

Translation: JPS 1985

---

* I.e., "Babylon"
‡ Heb. *balal* "confound," play on "Babel"

The Problem

There was one building supervisor at the Tower of Babel who spoke all languages, and he urged the other supervisors to allow him to coordinate the project. And he could have accomplished the task had the others agreed. So the problem wasn't mere semantics, even there.

G🙷 Abraham and Sarah

Genesis 11:31-32

³¹And Terah took Abram his son, and Lot the son of Haran, his son's son, and Sarai his daughter-in-law, his son Abram's wife; and they went forth with them from Ur of the Chaldees, to go into the land of Canaan; and they came unto Haran, and dwelt there. ³²And the days of Terah were two hundred and five years; and Terah died in Haran.🙷

The Call

It is clear from the text that the original call was to Abraham's father, Terah. And Terah responded to the call, and left his country, and his kindred and his father's house and departed from Ur of the Chaldees to go to the Promised Land, to Canaan. But when he came to Haran, he settled there. What happened? As one of Terah's descendants explained in another context: A sower went forth to sow; and when he sowed, some seed fell upon the stony places, some fell among thorns, and some fell on good ground.

Genesis 12:1-4

Now the LORD said unto Abram: 'Get thee out of thy country, and from thy kindred, and from thy father's house, unto the land that I will show thee. [2]And I will make of thee a great nation, and I will bless thee, and make thy name great; and be thou a blessing. [3]And I will bless them that bless thee, and him that curseth thee will I curse; and in thee shall all the families of the earth be blessed.' [4]So Abram went as the LORD had spoken unto him; and Lot went with him; and Abram was seventy and five years old when he departed out of Haran.✍

Before

When Abraham lived in Ur, he had a house, neighbors, a table, chairs, some grapes. Isn't this the prophet Zechariah's vision of the Messianic Age (3:10) when he foresees we will "call every man his neighbor under the vine"?

What did Abraham gain from his journeys to Haran, Canaan, and Egypt? He gained self-knowledge. He learned that he was a coward who could tell repeated lies about his wife and even betray her to other men when he felt his own life might be in danger. He learned that he could fail to prevent the destruction of entire cities, even though the person in power was willing to listen to his arguments and agree to whatever he dared to ask. He learned that he could sacrifice his lover and his sons if his wife, or some other figure to whom he'd ceded authority, insisted on it.

Was this self-knowledge worth the sacrifice of the millennial comforts Abraham had as a birthright in Ur? Couldn't Abraham appreciate sitting under a vine with his neighbor prior to his long and painful journey into self-knowledge? Of course not; it wouldn't have been the same vine.

Genesis 18:10-15

[10]And He said: 'I will certainly return unto thee when the season cometh round; and, lo, Sarah thy wife shall have a son.' And Sarah heard in the tent door, which was behind him.—[11]Now Abraham and Sarah were old, and well stricken in age; it had ceased to be with Sarah after the manner of women.— [12]And Sarah laughed within herself, saying: 'After I am waxed old shall I have pleasure, my lord being old also?' [13]And the LORD said unto Abraham: 'Wherefore did Sarah laugh, saying: Shall I of a surety bear a child, who am old? [14]Is any thing too hard for the LORD? At the set time I will return unto thee, when the season cometh round, and Sarah shall have a son.' [15]Then Sarah denied, saying: 'I laughed not'; for she was afraid. And He said: 'Nay; but thou didst laugh.'

Disbelief

When God told Abraham that Sarah, who was already ninety at the time, would have a child, she laughed. When God asked why she laughed, she became frightened and denied it. But Sarah shouldn't have worried; God doesn't mind disbelievers. God only gets annoyed if people are not attentive, and Sarah was listening intently.

H❧ The Righteous of Sodom

Genesis 18:23-33

[23]And Abraham drew near, and said: 'Wilt Thou indeed sweep away the righteous with the wicked? [24]Peradventure there are fifty righteous within the city; wilt Thou indeed sweep away and not forgive the place for the fifty righteous that are therein? [25]That be far from Thee to do after this manner, to slay the righteous with the wicked, that so the righteous should be as the wicked; that be far from Thee; shall not the Judge of all the earth do justly?' [26]And the LORD said: 'If I find in Sodom fifty righteous within the city, then I will forgive all the place for their sake.' [27]And Abraham answered and said: 'Behold now, I have taken upon me to speak unto the Lord, who am but dust and ashes. [28]Peradventure there shall lack five of the fifty righteous; wilt Thou destroy all the city for lack of five?' And He said: 'I will not destroy it, if I find there forty and five.' [29]And he spoke unto Him yet again, and said: 'Peradventure there shall be forty found there.' And He said: I will not do it for the forty's sake. [30]And he said: 'Oh, let not the Lord be angry, and I will speak. Peradventure there shall thirty be found there.' [31]And He said: 'I will not do it, if I find thirty there.' And he said: 'Behold now, I have taken upon me to speak unto the Lord. Peradventure there shall be twenty found there.' And He said: 'I will not destroy it for the twenty's sake.' [32]And he said: 'Oh, let not the Lord be angry, and I will speak yet but this once. Peradventure ten shall be found there.' And He said: 'I will not destroy it for the ten's sake.' [33]And the LORD went His way, as soon as He had left off speaking to Abraham; and Abraham returned unto his place.❧

Abstractions

Abraham was being disingenuous when he argued with God in an attempt to save the righteous of Sodom. His concern wasn't to save righteous people he didn't know—he didn't even know if these suppositions existed—but to save his nephew. It turned out that ten righteous people didn't in fact exist in Sodom, and this was where the bargaining stopped. But since God knew Abraham wasn't concerned with abstractions, God saved Lot anyhow.

I❧ Hagar and Ishmael

Genesis 21:14-19

[14]And Abraham arose up early in the morning, and took bread and a bottle of water, and gave it unto Hagar, putting it on her shoulder, and the child, and sent her away; and she departed, and strayed in the wilderness of Beersheba. [15]And the water in the bottle was spent, and she cast the child under one of the shrubs. [16]And she went, and sat her down over against him a good way off, as it were a bow-shot; for she said: 'Let me not look upon the death of the child.' And she sat over against him, and lifted up her voice, and wept. [17]And God heard the voice of the lad; and the angel of God called to Hagar out of heaven, and said unto her: 'What aileth thee, Hagar? fear not; for God hath heard the voice of the lad where he is. [18]Arise, lift up the lad, and hold him fast by thy hand; for I will make him a great nation.' [19]And God opened her eyes, and she saw a well of water; and she went, and filled the bottle with water, and gave the lad drink.❧

Cries and Tears

When Hagar and Ishmael were in the wilderness and the water had run out, she wept. "And God heard the voice of the lad." Hagar wept for a reason, a mother weeping for her dying child, while his cries were unknowing, merely a response to thirst. But, as we are told, his were the cries that were effective.

Why on earth hadn't Hagar seen the well before God pointed it out? Because her eyes were filled with tears. It was only after God had assured her Ishmael would be saved that she dried her tears and saw the well.

J∙ The Binding of Isaac

Genesis 22:1-9

And it came to pass after these things, that God did prove Abraham, and said unto him: 'Abraham'; and he said: 'Here am I.' ²And He said: 'Take now thy son, thine only son, whom thou lovest, even Isaac, and get thee into the land of Moriah; and offer him there for a burnt-offering upon one of the mountains which I will tell thee of.' ³And Abraham rose early in the morning, and saddled his ass, and took two of his young men with him, and Isaac his son; and he cleaved the wood for the burnt-offering, and rose up, and went unto the place of which God had told him. ⁴On the third day Abraham lifted up his eyes, and saw the place afar off. ⁵And Abraham said unto his young men: 'Abide ye here with the ass, and I and the lad will go yonder; and we will worship, and come back to you.' ⁶And Abraham took the wood of the burnt-offering, and laid it upon Isaac his son; and he took in his hand the fire and the knife; and they went both of them together. ⁷And Isaac spoke unto Abraham his father, and said: 'My father.' And he said: 'Here am I, my son.' And he said: 'Behold the fire and the wood; but where is the lamb for a burnt-offering?' ⁸And Abraham said: 'God will *provide Himself the lamb for a burnt-offering, my son.' So they went both of them together. ⁹And they came to the place which God had told him of; and Abraham built the altar there, and laid the wood in order, and bound Isaac his son, and laid him on the altar, upon the wood.∙

* Heb. *jireh;* that is, see for Himself

Moral Judgments

Abraham argued with God in an attempt to save the righteous of Sodom. Why didn't he argue with God in an attempt to save Isaac's life? He must have sensed one of these Divine decisions was meant more seriously than the other, but we don't know his thoughts and so have no means of judging Abraham's actions in moral terms.

Genesis 22:10-13

[10]And Abraham stretched forth his hand, and took the knife to slay his son. [11]And the angel of the LORD called unto him out of heaven, and said: 'Abraham, Abraham.' And he said: 'Here am I.' [12]And he said: "Lay not thy hand upon the lad, neither do thou any thing unto him; for now I know that thou art a God-fearing man, seeing thou hast not withheld thy son, thine only son, from Me.' [13]And Abraham lifted up his eyes, and looked, and behold behind him a ram caught in the thicket by his horns. And Abraham went and took the ram, and offered him up for a burnt-offering in the stead of his son.❧

The Offer

After sacrificing the ram, Abraham and Isaac descended from Mount Moriah. On the way down Isaac, still surprised, remarked, "So you really did intend to sacrifice me." Abraham considered denying it but decided to remain silent. After all, he wasn't being asked a question. He had, however, misunderstood Isaac. The echo of that mountain pass returned the faint response of a shy offer—"sacrifice me"—but Abraham was too preoccupied to hear it.

K➤ *After Sarah's Death*

Genesis 23:7-18

⁷And Abraham rose up, and bowed down to the people of the land, even to the children of Heth. ⁸And he spoke with them, saying: 'If it be your mind that I should bury my dead out of my sight, hear me, and entreat for me to Ephron the son of Zohar, ⁹that he may give me the cave of Machpelah, which he hath, which is in the end of his field; for the full price let him give it to me in the midst of you for a possession of a burying-place.' ¹⁰Now Ephron was sitting in the midst of the children of Heth; and Ephron the Hittite answered Abraham in the hearing of the children of Heth, even of all that went in at the gate of his city, saying: ¹¹'Nay, my lord, hear me: the field give I thee, and the cave that is therein, I give it thee; in the presence of the sons of my people give I it thee; bury thy dead.' ¹²And Abraham bowed down before the people of the land. ¹³And he spoke unto Ephron in the hearing of the people of the land, saying: 'But if thou wilt, I pray thee, hear me: I will give the price of the field; take it of me, and I will bury my dead there.' ¹⁴And Ephron answered Abraham, saying unto him: ¹⁵'My lord, hearken unto me: a piece of land worth four hundred shekels of silver, what is that betwixt me and thee? bury therefore thy dead.' ¹⁶And Abraham hearkened unto Ephron; and Abraham weighed to Ephron the silver, which he had named in the hearing of the children of Heth, four hundred shekels of silver, current money with the merchant. ¹⁷So the field of Ephron, which was in Machpelah, which was before Mamre, the field, and the cave which was therein, and all the trees that were in the field, that were in all the border thereof round about, were made sure ¹⁸unto Abraham for a possession in the presence of the children of Heth, before all that went in at the gate of his city.➤

Payment

When Abraham was informed that he was to possess the land of Israel, God forgot to mention it would have to be paid for. Perhaps God regarded as obvious the notion that you don't just take what belongs to others, although Joshua and the rest of humanity before and after have certainly thought they could.

We know Abraham had a sizable and effective private army, and that four local kings were under obligation to him for favors rendered in their hour of need. He could have taken the Cave of Machpelah by force if he'd wanted to. But he didn't, and he also didn't argue that, since God had promised him the entire land, the cave was his. Instead, Abraham acted as if it was important to acquire the land in a manner regarded as legitimate by the inhabitants. He actually begged the inhabitants for the right to purchase the land, and then accepted without bargaining a price that all commentators agree was very high, and his reputation did not suffer.

How the commentators arrived at the idea that the price was high I don't know. If the plot was unique in the eyes of either the buyer or the seller, then there could have been no market value established by the laws of supply and demand. We know from the Midrash that Adam and Eve were buried there, and can we doubt that Abraham also knew this? And what landowner in the Middle East would not know who was buried on his own property, or be so bad at bargaining that he couldn't sense the anxiety of the buyer sitting in front of him? So Abraham begged, and was happy to get the cave at the price he paid.

Genesis 25:1-4

And Abraham took another wife, and her name was Keturah. ²And she bore him Zimran, and Jokshan, and Medan, and Midian, and Ishbak, and Shuah. ³And Jokshan begot Sheba, and Dedan. And the sons of Dedan were Asshurim, and Letushim, and Leummim. ⁴And the sons of Midian: Ephah, and Epher, and Hanoch, and Abida, and Eldaah. All these were the children of Keturah.

Family Secrets

We are told that at the end of his life "Abraham took another wife, and her name was Keturah." Tradition tells us that Keturah was none other than Hagar.

Abraham kept in touch with Hagar and Ishmael after he expelled them from his home, which was also their home. It can now be safely revealed that Abraham made many secret trips to see Hagar and Ishmael while Sarah was alive. To what may this be compared? To the secret meetings between high Israeli officials and neighboring kings and potentates during the long years when this was publicly forbidden.

L⬥ Jacob's Ladder

Genesis 28:10-12

[10]And Jacob went out from Beersheba, and went toward Haran. [11]And he lighted upon the place, and tarried there all night, because the sun was set; and he took one of the stones of the place, and put it under his head, and lay down in that place to sleep. [12]And he dreamed, and behold a ladder set up on the earth, and the top of it reached to heaven; and behold the angels of God ascending and descending on it.⬥

The View from Jacob's Ladder

In his dream Jacob was curious enough to follow the angels as they climbed up the ladder. He followed them rung by rung through a cloud until they came to the top of the ladder, which was a platform wide enough for him to pause and take in the view before turning around and descending back toward earth again.

Had the ladder really reached to heaven, Jacob would not have been allowed to climb it even in a dream, for the true heavenly perspective is not permitted to mortals, as Job was told. We can, nonetheless, climb above the mundane from time to time and bring back with us this angelic perspective when we descend again into our daily lives.

Climbing Jacob's Ladder

Genesis 28:12 records what may be the world's best known dream and, as the Talmud observes (Berekhot 55b), "A dream uninterpreted is a letter unread."

I EMOTIONAL STATES

The dream is a projection of Jacob's emotional states. Jacob dreams about going up to heaven, then down in the opposite direction, then up to heaven and then down again, and so on. This is a dream, if there ever was one, of a manic-depressive:

Manic, as it is said in Genesis 29:20, reporting on an extended manic episode:

> And Jacob served seven years for Rachel; and they seemed unto him but a few days . . .

Depressive, as it is said in Genesis 47:8-9:

> And Pharaoh said unto Jacob, How old art thou?

> And Jacob said unto Pharoah, The days of the years
> of my pilgrimage are an hundred and thirty years: few
> and evil have the days of the years of my life been,
> and have not attained unto the days of the years of the
> life of my fathers in the days of their pilgrimage.

II EXISTENCE

Jacob's dream is to be interpreted in the light of Genesis 3:19:

> unto dust shalt thou return

This is to be understood in the light of two lines from quatrain XXIV of Fitzgerald's translation of the Rubaiyat:

> Ah, make the most of what we yet may spend
> Before we too into the Dust descend.

Therefore, the dream represents our lives, in which we ascend out of the dust of nonexistence up to the heaven of existence, and descend eventually back into the dust.

III MERCY

As it is said in Exodus 33:18-19:

> And [Moses] said: "Show me, I pray Thee, Thy glory." And
> [God] said: . . . "I will be gracious to whom I will be gracious,
> and will show mercy to whom I will show mercy."

Therefore the angels ascending represent those people to whom
grace and mercy have been shown. Some rise one rung, and some rise
ten rungs, and some rise even higher.

And the angels descending represent those people to whom mercy
has not been shown. Some descend one rung, and some ten rungs, and
some, such as those in the death camps fifty years ago or caught up in
tortures today, descend even more into hell "on the earth."

IV EFFECTS

A verse from afar:

> Verily, verily, I say unto you, Hereafter ye shall see heaven
> open, and the angels of God ascending and descending upon
> the Son of Man. [The Gospel According to John, 1:51.]

This verse is a powerful use of the imagery of Jacob's dream. The
angels represent those who have ascended or descended "upon" Jesus
or, in other words, by means of his life and words. This interpretation
can be easily generalized. Every individual influences others by words
and deeds. After all, we speak of "raising" children. Each of us is represented by the ladder. The effect on others of some of our words and
acts is elevating, and the effect of some of our words and acts is
depressing. And so Jacob's dream is a dream of the effects of the self on
others.

V ASSENT

Following the rabbis of the Midrash, who loved puns, do not read
only "ascending," but also "assenting." And do not only read
"descending," but also "dissenting."

As it is said by Dante in the *Inferno*, Canto iii, lines 58-60; Dante is
being shown around hell, and speaks:

> After I had recognized some amongst them
> I saw and knew the shadow of him who
> from cowardice made the great refusal.

Therefore the angels descending represent those individuals who in their lives made the great refusal, the great dissent. And those ascending represent the individuals who in their lives made the great affirmation, the great assent.

VI THE HEART

As it is said by Yeats in "The Circus Animals' Desertion," a late poem:

> I must lie down where all the ladders start
> in the foul rag and bone shop of the heart.

A rag and bone shop in Ireland in the early part of the century was one that sold decomposable material, like old rags and bones, for fertilizer, which is of course spread on the earth. [The shop is "foul" because of the smell.]

Let us decompose or, if you prefer, deconstruct Yeats' couplet in order to show its applicability to Jacob's dream:

I must lie down, as it is said (Genesis 28:11) "and he lay down in that place to sleep."

where all the ladders start, as it is said "and behold a ladder set up."

the foul rag and bone shop, as it is said "on the earth."

of the heart, as it is said (Deuteronomy 8:2) "to know what was in your heart."

Therefore the ladder is a projection of what is in the heart, and the angels are the feelings, the emotions, that are in the heart, that in some cases raise us up toward our aspirations and in other cases drag us down in the other direction.

Jacob's dream is a dream of the vicissitudes of the heart.

VII SUCCESS

Consider Jacob's situation. This is his first night out of the parental home. The whole world is before him, and the whole of his adult life. What would a young man dream of under these conditions? Success! What else? Jacob dreamed of climbing the ladder of success, of getting to the top, of rising to the highest position, of storming the heavens themselves. And he had many fantasies along these lines, each represented by an angel. This accounts for the first half of the dream.

But Jacob was a pampered child, and had lived a very sheltered and secure life up to that time. So he must have had his fears. Thoughts of successs must have immediately triggered fears of failure, of falling down on the job, or, as the dream-work so elegantly visualized it, of descending the ladder of success. This accounts for the second half of the dream, which is Jacob's dream of the hopes and fears associated with making it.

VIII LOVE

Consider Jacob's situation. This is his first night out of the parental home. The whole world is before him, and the whole of his adult life. What would a young man dream of under these conditions? Love! What else?

Jacob dreamed that he would meet the woman of his dreams and be transported to heaven. This accounts for the first half of the dream.

And now we come to a serious interpretive difficulty. If this is Jacob's dream of love, what are we to make of the second half of the dream under this interpretation?

We are in need of assistance from a proof-text. For example, Yeats' lines:

> All true love must die,
> Alter at the best
> Into some lesser thing.
> *Prove that I lie.*
>   "Words for Music Perhaps," section X

With this proof-text in mind we can look carefully at such evidence as exists concerning Jacob's love for Rachel in the latter years of their marriage.

Rachel's death is described in these terms (Genesis 35:17-19):

> And it came to pass, when she was in hard labour that the midwife said unto her, Fear not; thou shalt have this son also.

> And it came to pass, as her soul was in departing, (for she died) that she called his name Ben-oni [that is, son of my sorrow]: but his father called him Benjamin [that is, son of the right hand].

And Rachel died, and was buried on the way to Ephrath . . .

Now let us do some arithmetic. Jacob was 130 when he was introduced to Pharaoh, and we know that at the time Benjamin was still young, surely no more than twenty. So Jacob must have been 110 at a minimum when he got Rachel pregnant for the second time. This is an impressive feat, and I'm confident that everyone will be able to identify fully with Jacob's pride in the continued vigor of his "right hand."

So Jacob brushed aside Rachel's poignant last wish to have the child named in remembrance of her death throes, a wish which was uttered with her dying breath. And Jacob named the child to commemorate his right hand or, to be pedantically accurate, the right hand in general. And Jacob buried Rachel by the side of the road, and moved on.

If we assume that there was indeed a certain loss of love in the marriage, then the second half of the dream can be interpreted as a decline from the heavenly intensity of true love to what Yeats called "some lesser thing," and the dream is then Jacob's dream of love.

IX CLEAN HANDS

As it is said (Psalm 24:3-4):

> Who shall ascend into the mountain of the Lord?
> and who shall stand in his holy place?
> He that hath clean hands, and a pure heart;

So the angels ascending represent those with clean hands and a pure heart.

And what about those descending? This is to be understood with the aid of a proof-text from afar (Ephesians 4:10): "He that descended is the same also that ascended." Therefore the dream teaches us that even if you have clean hands and a pure heart you will eventually descend from your heaven and join the rest of us here on earth.

X SOJOURN

As it is said (Psalm 39:13):

> Hear my prayer, O Lord,
>   and give ear unto my cry;
>   Keep not silence at my tears;
> For I am a stranger with Thee,
>   A sojourner, as all my fathers were.

Therefore the dream teaches us that even if we rise up to heaven, so to speak, in our lives, the stay will be brief, a sojourn before we descend again, for we are stangers there.

Jacob's dream was of the transience of our elevations, our ascents, the transience of our moments of joy and happiness.

XI CONNECTION

As it is said (Psalm 139:8):

> If I ascend into heaven, Thou art there;
>   If I make my bed in the netherworld, behold, Thou
>   art there.

So the dream teaches us that in both our ascents and descents we are in the same circumstances, that even in our descents we are still on a ladder connecting our heaven and earth: we are still in contact with whatever permitted us to ascend.

XII A DIFFICULT EQUILIBRIUM

As it is said, by Kafka, in perhaps the greatest parable of the twentieth century:

> He is a free and secure citizen of the world, for he is fettered to a chain which is long enough to give him the freedom of all earthly space, and yet only so long that nothing can drag him past the frontiers of the world. But simultaneously he is a free and secure citizen of Heaven as well, for he is also fettered by a similarly designed heavenly chain. So if he heads, say, for the earth, his heavenly collar throttles him, and if he heads for Heaven, his earthly one does the same. And yet all the possibilities are his, and he feels it; more, he actually refuses to account for the deadlock by an error in the original fettering.

Therefore Jacob's dream teaches us that if we head for heaven we will eventually feel stifled in that rarified atmosphere, and descend back toward earth again in order to breathe. And if we go too far in this reversal we will eventually try to turn around, to rise out of the mud.

And so the dream teaches us that our spiritual double binds are due to the original fettering. We feel free, and are free, but we are constructed to feel ill at ease if we move too far in either spiritual direction. Our existential situation, in other words, is designed to produce thoughtful neurotics.

XIII INVITATION

As it is said in *Pesikta de-Rab Kahana* 23:2:

> The Holy One said: "Jacob, climb thou also." . . . But Jacob . . . did not climb up.

The consequences of such passive refusal are to be understood in the light of the following lines from Shakespeare (*Julius Caesar*, IV, iii, 49-53):

> There is a tide in the affairs of men,
> Which, taken at the flood, leads on to fortune;
> Omitted, all the voyage of their life
> Is bound in shallows and in miseries.

"Omitted" is a passive refusal. This teaches us that if we are ever invited in our lives to ascend some Jacob's ladder, we should accept.

XIV ENCHANTMENT

> And he dreamed, and behold a ladder set up on the earth, and the top of it reached to heaven: and behold the angels of God ascending and descending on it.

This dream is to be understood in the light of the following line from one of Yeats' last poems:

> It was the dream itself enchanted me.

M🨂 *Rachel*

Genesis 31:17-19

[17]Thereupon Jacob put his children and wives on camels; [18]and he drove off all his livestock and all the wealth that he had amassed, the livestock in his possession that he had acquired in Paddan-aram, to go to his father Isaac in the land of Canaan.

[19]Meanwhile Laban had gone to shear his sheep, and Rachel stole her father's household idols.🨂

Translation: JPS 1985

Beauty

Why did Rachel steal the idols? Was one of the matriarchs an idol worshipper? Surely not! But she was lovely and, as we know from our excavations, the idols were lovely too. We display them in our museums, and why should Rachel have been less sensitive to beauty than we are?

N. At the Ford of the Jabbok

Genesis 32:23-24

[23]And he rose up that night, and took his two wives, and his two handmaids, and his eleven children, and passed over the ford of the Jabbok. [24]And he took them, and sent them over the stream, and sent over that which he had.

Encumbrances

Jacob sent his wives, children, and possessions across the ford of the river Jabbok in order to be alone. All his great visions had, in the past, come to him while he was alone on his journey, and he knew encumbrances had to be put aside if he was to receive another encounter, and he knew he had need of one.

²⁵And Jacob was left alone; and there wrestled a man with him until the breaking of the day. ²⁶And when he saw that he prevailed not against him, he touched the hollow of his thigh; and the hollow of Jacob's thigh was strained, as he wrestled with him. ²⁷And he said: 'Let me go, for the day breaketh.' And he said: 'I will not let thee go, except thou bless me.' ²⁸And he said unto him: 'What is thy name?' And he said: 'Jacob.' ²⁹And he said: 'Thy name shall be called no more Jacob, but Israel*; for thou hast striven with God and with men, and hast prevailed.' ³⁰And Jacob asked him, and said: 'Tell me, I pray thee, thy name.' And he said: 'Wherefore is it that thou dost ask after my name?' And he blessed him there.

* That is, *He who striveth with God.*

Three Old Symbols

The wound-up thread he held played out until
Theseus found, within his maze, the beast he had to kill.

Shiva, dancing in a ring of flame,
treads down the demon that his dance must tame.

In darkness Jacob wrestled with a stranger who
did not prevail, and blessed him, when their night was through.

O⤳ The Burning Bush

Exodus 3:13-14

¹³And Moses said unto God: 'Behold, when I come unto the children of Israel, and shall say unto them: The God of your fathers hath sent me unto you; and they shall say to me: What is His name? what shall I say unto them?' ¹⁴And God said unto Moses: 'I AM THAT I AM'; and He said: 'Thus shalt thou say unto the children of Israel: I AM hath sent me unto you.⤳

An Onion

Sure, there's an outer skin
but when that's quickly peeled
(and it's only brittle and thin)
true onion is revealed.

An onion that could speak
would say *ad nauseam*
you've nothing more to seek,
just see: I am what I am.

Exodus 4:27-28

[27]And the LORD said to Aaron: 'Go into the wilderness to meet Moses.' And he went, and met him in the mountain of God, and kissed him. [28]And Moses told Aaron all the words of the LORD wherewith He had sent him, and all the signs wherewith He had charged him.➣

The Chosen

A few days after Aaron arrived in Midian, Moses took him out to the wilderness near Mount Horeb to show him the thornbush from which the Voice had spoken. Moses understood it would no longer be burning without being consumed but still somehow expected to recognize the bush that had been chosen. Perhaps he thought a halo would surround it, an afterglow of the Presence. Perhaps it was some residual idolatry from his Egyptian upbringing. In any case, of course, no such sign was evident, and he couldn't distinguish that particular bush from all the others.

P. *The Exodus*

Exodus 4:29-31 and 12:37-39

²⁹And Moses and Aaron went and gathered together all the elders of the children of Israel. ³⁰And Aaron spoke all the words which the LORD had spoken unto Moses, and did the signs in the sight of the people. ³¹And the people believed; and when they heard that the LORD had remembered the children of Israel, and that He had seen their affliction, then they bowed their heads and worshipped . . . ³⁷And the Children of Israel journeyed from Ramses to Succoth, about six hundred thousand men on foot, beside children. ³⁸And a mixed multitude went up also with them; and flocks, and herds, even very much cattle. ³⁹And they baked unleavened cakes of the dough which they brought forth out of Egypt, for it was not leavened; because they were thrust out of Egypt, and could not tarry, neither had they prepared for themselves any victual.

Rational Choice

Moses proposed to the Children of Israel that they leave Egypt, the cradle of civilization, and follow him into the wilderness. Since he'd made no provision for shelter, it's understandable that there were Hebrews in Egypt, mostly those holding supervisory positions, who chose not to leave.

They refused to be part of a stampeded populace led by a mad stuttering murderer who discoursed in the desert with burning bushes. They expected the worst, including the worship of golden calves. They stayed civilized slaves and so did not experience the separation of the Sea, or the pillar of cloud guiding by day, or the pillar of fire guiding by night, or the rock that gushed water when Moses struck it, or the gathering of the manna, or the Voice over Sinai, or the countenance of Moses descending the mountain.

Exodus 14:10-13 and 22

[10]And when Pharoah drew nigh, the children of Israel lifted up their eyes, and, behold, the Egyptians were marching after them; and they were sore afraid; and the children of Israel cried out unto the LORD. [11]And they said unto Moses: 'Because there were no graves in Egypt, hast thou taken us away to die in the wilderness? wherefore hast thou dealt thus with us, to carry us forth out of Egypt? [12]Is not this the word that we did tell thee in Egypt, saying, Let us alone, that we may serve the Egyptians? For it were better for us to serve the Egyptians, than that we should die in the wilderness.' [13]And Moses said unto the people: 'Fear ye not, stand still, and see the salvation of the LORD, which he will work for you to-day; for whereas ye have seen the Egyptians to-day, ye shall see them again no more for ever.'

. . .

[22]And the children of Israel went into the midst of the sea upon the dry ground; and the waters were a wall unto them on their right hand, and on their left.

At the Sea of Reeds

It is said:

In each generation we exodus from Egypt,
reach the Sea of Reeds, look back in fear,
and protest to whoever led us there:
Why bring us to this desert just to die!
We'll kill ourselves by drowning in the sea!
We'll return to slavery and escape annihilation!
We'll fight the forces of enslavement unaided!
We'll shout, frighten them with noise!

But that generation—so goes another midrash—
stopped their complaint against circumstance
and entered those waters up to their toes,
up to their ankles, up to their knees,
up to their lips, up to their nostrils,
and only then did the miracle occur.

²³And when they came to Marah, they could not drink of the waters of Marah, for they were bitter. Therefore the name of it as called Marah* ²⁴And the people murmured against Moses, saying: 'What shall we drink?' ²⁵And he cried unto the LORD; and the LORD showed him a tree, and he cast it into the waters, and the waters were made sweet.

* That is, *Bitterness.*

Sundry Lessons of the Exodus

Something will guide you; if not fire, a cloud.

You're a mixed multitude, don't be too proud.

You'll be pursued by what you leave behind.

This wilderness is where you'll be divined.

The water here is bitter; make it sweet.

Eat the strange food; it's all you have to eat.

You can't turn back, of course. And can't forget.

And did escape. Why keep that amulet?

line 1: Exodus 13:21-22
line 2: see page 64
line 3: see page 66
line 4: see page 70
line 6: Exodus 16:4-36

Q❧ The Lord Thy God

Exodus 20:1-3

And God spoke all these words saying:

[2]I am the LORD thy God, who brought thee out of the land of Egypt, out of the house of bondage.

[3]Thou shalt have no other gods before Me.❧

Interpretations of "I Am the Lord Thy God"

I THE IMAGINATIVE NECESSITY OF GOD

The phrase "I am the Lord thy God" is to be understood as an asertion of existence: "I, the Lord thy God, am." And this assertion is to be understood in the light of Voltaire's well-known remark:

> If God didn't exist we would have to invent him.

There are some things that can only be said by addressing God, or having God speak. The Yiddish poet Jacob Glatstein, for example, addressed God in this passage from his poem "Genesis," as translated by Cynthia Ozick:

> We've both turned universal.
> Come back, dear God, to a land
>   no bigger than a speck.
> Dwindle down to only ours.
> I'll go around with homely sayings
> suitable for chewing over in small places.
> We'll both be provincial.
> God and His poet.
> Maybe it will go sweeter for us.

And no one but God could have said what Alain Bosquet puts into His mouth (in French, as translated by Jesse Abbot):

> God speaks:
> "I'm not always fond of what I create.
> For instance, this man . . ."

II THE NAME AND NATURE OF GOD

The phrase "I am the Lord thy God" is to be understood as an indication of God's name and nature: "I am [is] the Lord thy God." Exodus 3:14 is the proof-text:

> And God said unto Moses: "I AM THAT I AM;"
> and He said: "Thus shalt thou say unto the children
> of Israel: I AM hath sent me unto you."

So one of God's names, indicative of His nature, is "I AM" or (in the standard scholarly gloss) "I WILL BE," since the Hebrew verb is in the imperfect. If the believer's God is immanent as well as transcendent, this interpretation is quite consistent with belief. To a nonbeliever, this interpretation would be metapsychological: there is a core of being (or Being) within us which can act as our standard of authenticity and guide. As it is said (in the *Dhammapada*, verse 221):

Let a man put away anger, let him forsake pride,
let him overcome all bondage!

We can be brought out of bondage to the inauthentic in ourselves. Buddha, the author of the remarks just quoted, told of his Way. And Freud had his analysis ("Where Id is there Ego shall be.") for bringing us out of enslavement to slave-masters within. As it is said (in the Gospel according to Luke, 17:21):

The Kingdom of Heaven is within you.

III THE GOD OF THE ANCIENT TEXTS

Voltaire had no need to strain his powers of invention. A vast body of writings record acts and words attributed to God and His representatives, and interpretations of these words and acts. The "homely sayings" in these writings are our heritage, and believers and nonbelievers alike can bring their own agendas to them, as others did in their day, and as anyone who feels the necessity can do in our own. There are arguments and lamentations and prayers and stories and proverbs and protests in the ancient texts, and all those who allow their imagination to be shaped by them will, of necessity, encounter their God.

The God of Semitic Monotheism
Interpretations of "I am the Lord Thy God."
Prooftexts from the Koran

I THE CHILDREN OF ISRAEL

A verse from afar. As it is said in the Koran, Sura 2, with God speaking:

> Children of Israel, remember My blessing
> wherewith I blessed you, and that I
> have preferred you above all beings.

Here, "the Lord thy God," refers to a God who chose the Children of Israel, who preferred them, in the Koran's formulation, to all other beings.

II BELIEF

A verse from afar. As it is said, in the Koran, Sura 7, with God speaking in the royal plural of the visit of Moses and Aaron to Pharaoh and his sorcerers, and the incident with the snakes (Exodus 7:8-13):

> And We revealed to Moses: 'Cast thy staff.'
> And lo, it forthwith swallowed up their lying invention.
> . . .
> And the sorcerers were cast down, bowing themselves.
> They said, 'We believe in the Lord of all Being,
> the Lord of Moses and Aaron.'
> Said Pharaoh [to the sorcerers], "You have believed in Him
> before I gave you leave."

Why is Pharaoh's statement an absurdity? Because belief is subjective, personal to each individual, and cannot be controlled by any dictator. Here, God's revelation is directly to each individual, even Pharaoh's sorcerers, and is not mediated by a Pharaoh or anyone else. As it is said, "I am the Lord *thy* God."

III THE UNIVERSAL

A verse from afar. As it is said, in the Koran, Sura 2:

> And they say, 'None shall enter Paradise
> except that they be Jews or Christians.'
> Such are their fancies. Say [to them]: 'Produce
> your proof, if you speak truly.'
>
> Nay, but whosoever submits his will to God . . .
> his wage is with his Lord[.]

And Exodus Rabbah V:9, refering to what happened when God spoke "all these words," tells us:

> R. Yohanan said: "God's voice, as it was uttered split up into seventy voices, so that all the nations should understand."

Therefore, "the Lord thy God" refers to a God whose revelation is universal, and in the separate languages, and by extension the figurative usages and imagery, of each culture.

IV REFUGE

A verse from afar. As it is said, in the Koran, Sura 114, the last in the Koran, entitled "Men," possibly with generic intent:

> In the Name of God, the Merciful, the Compassionate
> Say: "I take refuge with the Lord of men,
> the King of men,
> the God of men,
>
> from the evil of the slinking whisperer
> who whispers in the hearts of men
> of jinn and men."

I imagine this is the same slinking whisperer who dictates Freudian slips and, in some, more violent messages. This is to be understood in the light of Psalm 7:2:

> O Lord my God, in Thee have I taken refuge;
> Save me from all them that pursue me, and deliver me;
> Lest he tear my soul like a lion,
> Rending it in pieces . . .

Here, "the Lord thy God" refers to a God with whom believers can take refuge from the enemies of their soul, from the slinking whisperer who whispers in their hearts.

V   WISDOM

A verse from afar. As it is said, in the Koran, Sura 108:

> In the Name of God, the Merciful, the Compassionate:
>   Surely We have given thee abundance;
>
> . . .
>
>   Surely he that hates thee, he is the one cut off.

The last line is not a truth of social or political life, but it is a truth of the inner life, a truth of subjective experience. Now, Proverbs 8:36, in which a personified Wisdom is speaking, tells us:

> They that sin against me wrong their own soul

This is to be understood in the light of Job, chapter 38, verse 36, in which God, by means of a rhetorical question, says in effect:

> I have put wisdom in the inward parts

I take this to mean that wisdom is an attribute of the natural order. True wisdom expresses a law of Nature. Wise statements pertain to the realm of facts not values. Here, "the Lord thy God" refers to a God who made it one of the laws of the inner life that hatred cuts off the one who hates, that those who sin against the logic of this Wisdom wrong their own souls.

VI   THE RIGHTEOUS

A verse from afar. As it is said in the Koran, Sura 7:

> None feels secure against God's devising
>   but the people of the lost.

This is to be understood in the light of the following, from Genesis Rabbah:

> Psalm 11:5 states "The Lord tests the righteous." Rabbi Yohanan explained: "A potter does not test defective vessels." Rabbi Eleazar said: "When a man has two oxen, one strong and the other feeble, upon which does he put the yoke? Surely on the strong one."

Here, "the Lord thy God" refers to a God who tries the righteous, who puts a yoke on those who can bear it, a God with whom none feels secure, except those who are lost.

VII OUR PORTION

A verse from afar. As it is said in the Koran, Sura 5:

> Surely We sent down the Torah, wherein is
> guidance and light; thereby the Prophets
> who had surrended themselves gave judgement
> for those of Jewry, as did the masters
> and the rabbis, following such portion
> of God's Book as they were given to keep
> and were witnesses to.

Here, "the Lord thy God" refers to a God who gave the Children of Israel that portion of the Book which was theirs to keep, and to which they are witnesses. This is of quite general applicability: To others, other fates; to us, whoever we are, our portion.

VIII MINDS

A verse from afar. As it is said in the Koran, Sura 40:

> We also gave Moses the guidance,
> and We bequeathed upon the Children
> of Israel the Book for a guidance
> and for a reminder to men possessed of minds.

As it is said: "I am the Lord thy God, who brought thee out of the Land of Egypt, out of the House of Bondage." This refers to a God who expects devotees to look in the Book for guidance and reminders, but not to be slaves, to use their minds in interpreting its messages.

IX THE ABODE

A verse from afar. As it is said in the Koran, Sura 38:

> Remember also Our servants Abraham,
> Isaac and Jacob—men of might they and of vision.
> Assuredly We purified them with a
> quality most pure, the remembrance of the Abode[.]

Now, Isaiah tells us in chapter 6, verse 1:

> In the year that king Uzziah died I saw the Lord
> sitting upon a throne high and lifted up, and his train filled the
> temple. Above him stood the seraphim . . . And one called to
> another and said: "Holy, holy, holy, is the Lord of Hosts. . . ."

As it is said, in the *Dhammapada,* couplet 114:

> Compared to a life of one hundred years of not seeing the immortal place, one day is better if in it we see the immortal place.

Here, "the Lord thy God" refers to a God who permits some creatures to see the Abode, the Throne, the immortal place.

X   ABRAHAM'S CHILDREN

A verse from afar. As it is said in the Koran, Sura 2:

> Say you: 'We believe in God, and
> in that which has been sent down on us
> and sent down on Abraham, Ishmael,
> Isaac and Jacob, and the Tribes[.]'

Here, "the Lord thy God" refers to the God of Abraham, and Isaac and Ishmael. As it is said, in Genesis 25:9, speaking of the death of Abraham:

> And his sons Isaac and Ishmael buried him in the cave of Machpelah.

XI   MESSENGERS

A verse from afar. As it is said, in the Koran, Sura 4:

> We have revealed to thee as We revealed
> to Noah, and the Prophets after him,
> and We revealed to Abraham, Ishmael,
> Isaac, Jacob, and the Tribes,
> Jesus and Job, Jonah and Aaron,
> and Solomon, and We gave David Psalms,
> and Messengers We have already told thee of
> before, and Messengers We have not told thee of[.]

Here, "the Lord thy God" refers to the God of Abraham and Isaac and Jacob and Ishmael and Jesus. And the God of all the other Messengers we have been told of, such as Devorah and Hagar. And the God of all the Messengers we do not know about.

XII FOUNTAINS

A verse from afar. As it is said, in the Koran, Sura 2:

> And when Moses sought water for his people,
> So We said, 'Strike with thy staff the rock;'
> and there gushed forth from it twelve fountains;
> all the people knew now their drinking place.

Here, "the Lord thy God" refers to a God that provides fountains or drinking places in the wilderness for the twelve tribes. There is a hint of the metaphoric here. If so, the text is implying that these are fountains of a spiritual and permanent nature. Ben Jonson's lines come to mind:

> The thirst that from the soul doth rise,
>   doth ask a drink divine

Exodus 20:22-25

[19]And the LORD said unto Moses: Thus thou shalt say unto the children of Israel: Ye yourselves have seen that I have talked with you from heaven. [20]Ye shall not make with Me gods of silver, or gods of gold, ye shall not make unto you. [21]An altar of earth thou shalt make unto Me, and shalt sacrifice thereon thy burnt-offerings, and thy peace-offerings, thy sheep, and thine oxen; in every place where I cause My name to be mentioned I will come unto thee and bless thee. [22]And if thou make Me an altar of stone, thou shalt not build it of hewn stones; for if thou lift up thy tool upon it, thou hast profaned it.

Sacred Sites
[Exodus 20:25]

Mount Sinai isn't sacred; no one goes
on pilgrimage to see where Moses climbed
toward Torah. Why look at piles of rock?
Whatever went on there is now dispersed
among the nations. Yet the Western Wall
has crumbled to a site: its stones were hewn
by human fingers and retain their print
which may rub off, and so we fondle those
ancestral blocks as idolizers of
the sensible, failing to comprehend
what Yahweh had in mind when he said, *if
you make stone altars don't use hewn stone*
but, like your nomad ancestors, be sane,
build by the road from what you can pick up:
only what goes on is not a pile of rock.

R⋗ Offerings

Exodus 25:1-8

And the LORD spoke unto Moses, saying: [2]"Speak unto the children of Israel, that they take for Me an offering; of every man whose heart maketh him willing ye shall take My offering. [3]And this is the offering which ye shall take of them: gold, and silver, and brass; [4]and blue, and purple, and scarlet, and fine linen, and goats' hair; [5]and rams' skins dyed red, and sealskins, and acacia-wood; [6]oil for the light, spices for the anointing oil, and for the sweet incense; [7]onyx stones, and stones to be set, for the ephod, and for the breastplate. [8]And let them make Me a sanctuary, that I may dwell among them.[']⋗

Offerings

And the Lord spoke unto Moses, saying, 'Speak unto the
children of Israel, that they take for Me an offering[.']

[Exodus 25:1-2]

The key phrase, considered in isolation, is "take for Me an offering." Some ancient rabbinic interpretations transform the opening verse in a useful way by reading "for Me" as "Me for." The key phrase reads, in this variant, "take Me for an offering."

Can we playfully and willfully read into the key phrase some contemporary meanings of the notion of "an offering"? To do so, we will have to impute various identities to the speaker, represented by the word "Me."

I OF THE SELF TO THE BODY

The phrase "take for Me an offering" is to be understood in the light of Song of Songs 5:2, which reads:

> I sleep but my heart waketh

By the logic of our assumption, the words "my heart" and the "Me" of Exodus 25:1 are the same. But to what do the words "my heart" refer? Well, when I sleep my heart continues to function, it continues to beat. And not only my heart, but my whole autonomic nervous system. Not to put too fine a point on it, the verse from the Song of Songs means:

> I sleep but my body is awake.

And this is true: our body is indeed the unsleeping guardian of our Self, our spirit or, if you prefer, our soul. And so we should make offerings or sacrifices to ensure its well-being. We should, of course, stop smoking, and give up cheesecake, and crème brûlée. And we should set aside time each day to exercise. These are the offerings of our Self to the body for the sake of its well-being.

Now, coming back to Exodus 25:1 and understanding the key phrase in the light of our interpretation of Song of Songs 5:2, the word "Me" refers to the body and so the body is speaking, and I believe there is a veiled threat in the remark, *take for Me an offering*

II OF THE BODY TO THE SELF

As it is said:

I sleep but my heart waketh

To what do the words "my heart" refer? Well, when I sleep my heart continues to function, it continues to beat. And not only my heart but my whole autonomic nervous system or, not to put too fine a point on it:

I sleep but my body is awake.

This implies a duality, an opposition between the Self (or spirit or soul, as you prefer) and the body. Dialogs between the Body and the Self (or Soul) form a voluminous literature from the Renaissance on, and are part of an even larger literature of debates on the relative merits of the sacred and profane views of life. The sacred view, that life should be dedicated to a religious vocation to which all else is subordinate or even, if necessary, sacrificed, has a contemporary secular equivalent in lives dedicated to art or any other activity considered as a vocation.

To derive the idea of a life of vocation from our text, we need the rabbinic licence to read the text as "Take Me for an offering." In the light of our interpretation of Song of Songs 5:2, the word "Me" is the body conceived as that aspect of the human being subject to decay, that has a limited lifetime. The Self then demands of it, "Let me use you for the purpose of creating something that will live after me, art or poetry or the truths of science." The body responds,

Take Me—take my lifetime—*for an offering*

III OF THE MUNDANE TO THE DREAM

As it is said (Song of Songs 5:2): "I sleep but my heart waketh." To what do the words "my heart" refer? When I sleep, I dream. In other words, my dreams are awake. So, substitiuting "dreams" for "heart" the verse from the Song of Songs becomes "I sleep but my dreams are awake."

Now, Ecclesiastes 5:3 states:

A dream is the result of much business.

As a result of much business with the passing hour we may be able to save enough from our earnings to support our dream of artistic creation. That is, as a result of much business we can make an offering to our dream. As it is said, in Exodus 25:1, with our Dream speaking:

take for Me an offering

IV OF THE UNCONSCIOUS TO CONSCIOUSNESS

As it is said (Song of Songs 5:2): "I sleep but my heart waketh."

To what do the words "my heart" refer? When I sleep, I dream. In other words, my dreams are awake. So, substitiuting "dreams" for "heart" the verse from the Song of Songs becomes:

I sleep but my dreams are awake.

Now, the Talmud (Berekhot 55b) states:

A dream uninterpreted is a letter unread.

This agrees with the continuation of the verse from the Song of Songs 5:2:

I sleep but my [dreams] are awake
It is the voice of my beloved that knocks.

So, using the imagery of the Talmud, this is the unconscious as postman delivering dreams and saying, "Do I have a letter for you!" In Song of Songs 5:2 under this interpretation the unconscious continues to address the person sleeping, saying:

Open to me, my sister, my love,
for my head is filled with dew,
with the distillations of the night.

According to Freud and Jung and their followers, the interpretation of dreams, those "distillations of the night," is an act that has the potential to be spiritually efficacious. Bronze Age worshippers regarded their own offerings in the same way. Therefore, using the rabbinic misreading of the verse we are interpreting:

Let them take Me—the dream is speaking—*for an offering . . .*—to their psychoanalyst.

The continuation of our text from the opening of Exodus 25 is consistent with this interpretation. It specifies the two main preconditions for converting the potential of dream interpretation into an efficacious act:

Whosoever is of a willing heart let them bring it . . .

This agrees with the well-known requirements of psycho-analysis—there's no point in bringing a dream to an analyst unless you also bring a heart willing to accept the interpretation. Furthermore, the verse goes on:

Let them bring gold, silver . . .

As we all know, these or their equivalent are also essential.

V MATERIALITY

As it is said, by William Butler Yeats, in one of his last poems, "The Circus Animals' Desertion":

Players and the painted stage took all my love
and not those things that they were emblems of.

In other words, we are creatures who can be easily mistaken in the objects of our affection. We can even get distracted by baubles and trinkets, by jewelry and fine clothes, by trappings. Therefore, as our text says:

take for Me an offering.

In other words, offer up your baubles and trinkets:

And this is the offering which ye shall take of them: gold, and silver, and brass . . . and fine linen.

And this in turn is to be understood in the light of Confucius' remark in the *Analects*:

A square dish without corners, what sort of a square dish is that?

This wonderful tautology is, of course, directly applicable to our text:

An offering without sacrifice, what sort of an offering is that?

Therefore, with God speaking:

take for Me an offering

provided that it's made of gold, silver, or other valuable materials.

An offering must have a certain materiality, must entail a real sacrifice. No "gifts" of good will or prayer will do. This is in keeping with the spirit of rabbinic Judaism in which, for example, the commandment to visit the sick means getting up and doing it, not merely having them in your thoughts, or saying a prayer for their recovery.

VI   A RECEPTIVE MIND

To what may the phrase "Let them take for Me an offering" be compared? To a story from the Buddhist tradition:

> A monk is training a novice in meditation. He says: Go and sit comfortably somewhere and concentrate on your breath. Feel the breath leave your nostril; then feel it enter. Feel it leave; feel it enter. Do this for half an hour and come back and tell me your experiences.
>
> After ten minutes the novice rushes up to the monk in excitement and says, "I've just had a great spiritual experience, a communing with the Divine! I did what you said for five minutes and then, all of a sudden, I saw the Lord Buddha sitting on a golden lotus, and He leaned toward me and recited the whole first chapter of the *Dhammapada!*"
>
> The monk said, with irritation, "If you had resumed concentrating on your breath it would have gone away."

The novice was supposed to have had, for a few fleeting moments, the experience of a mind focused without distraction on one simple (and completely physical) awareness. And, of course, he was also supposed to begin learning how to bring his untrained mind back to its focus when it got distracted, even when the distraction seemed to take the form of a religious vision. In other words, the novice was supposed to learn to create in himself a still center, a quiescent and therefore receptive mind, in which meditation can be practiced and in which revelations can be received.

Applying this to our text, we can understand it to be God speaking in the capacity of Mentor to Israel in the novice phase of its religious life. God's command to the Children of Israel is then "Let them take for Me an offering" provided it is of gold, silver or other physical material they regard as precious. The Mentor of Israel then goes on to say, Let them build with these trinkets a place that will be a proper focus of their attention. As it is said, in Exodus 25:8:

> And let them make Me a sanctuary, that I may dwell among them.

S❧ Laws

Leviticus 1:1-5

The LORD called to Moses and spoke to him from the Tent of Meeting, saying: ²Speak to the Israelite people, and say to them:

> When any of you presents an offering of cattle to the LORD, *-he shall choose his-* offering from the herd, or from the flock.

³If his offering is a burnt offering from the herd, he shall make his offering a male without blemish. He shall bring it to the entrance of the Tent of Meeting, for acceptance in his behalf before the LORD. ⁴He shall lay his hand upon the head of the burnt offering, that it may be acceptable in his behalf, in expiation for him. ⁵The bull shall be slaughtered before the LORD; and Aaron's sons, the priests, shall offer the blood, dashing the blood against all sides of the altar which is at the entrance of the Tent of Meeting.❧

Translation: JPS 1985

- Lit. "you shall offer your."

Animal Sacrifice

Was there anything wrong with slaughtering animals as part of a religious ritual? The case in favor has been ably argued by D. H. Lawrence, in a poem entitled "The Old Idea of Sacrifice":

> [S]acrifice is the law of life which enacts
> that little lives must be eaten up into
>   the dance and splendour
> of bigger lives, with due reverence and acknowledgement.

Lawrence has presented a law of nature. Birds eat worms. And the worms are, by this means, bound into the splendor of the handsome, fuller life, and get to fly in the heavens, something worms can't do by themselves, and to make an absolutely essential contribution to the production of melodious sound. And if you were to argue that the worms had no such aspirations, I could respond the way the Voice Out of the Whirlwind did to Job, namely: what do worms know, anyhow?

¹³And every meal-offering of thine shalt thou season with salt; neither shalt thou suffer the salt of the covenant of thy God to be lacking from thy meal-offering; with all thine offerings thou shalt offer salt.➳

Salt

Why did God insist that all offerings should have salt on them? Did God need it as a preservative? Of course not. We are being instructed to make sure whatever we give to someone else has savor.

Leviticus 14:1-8

And the LORD spoke unto Moses, saying:

²This shall be the law of the leper in the day of his cleansing: he shall be brought unto the priest. ³And the priest shall go forth out of the camp; and the priest shall look, and, behold, if the plague of leprosy be healed in the leper; ⁴then shall the priest command to take for him that is to be cleansed two living clean birds, and cedar-wood, and scarlet, and hyssop. ⁵And the priest shall command to kill one of the birds in an earthen vessel over running water. ⁶As for the living bird, he shall take it, and the cedar-wood, and the scarlet, and the hyssop, and shall dip them and the living bird in the blood of the bird that was killed over the running water. ⁷And he shall sprinkle upon him that is to be cleansed from the leprosy seven times, and shall pronounce him clean, and shall let go the living bird into the open field. ⁸And he that is to be cleansed shall wash his clothes, and shave off all his hair, and bathe himself in water, and he shall be clean; and after that he may come into the camp, but shall dwell outside his tent seven days.

A Bird's Eye View*

That great but unknown rabbi, Ezra ben Zipporah, tells us that on one of the occasions when the ritual of cleansing the leper was performed, the bird that was dipped in the blood of the slaughtered bird and then released was named Horace. Scholars may be inclined to deduce from this that Ben Zipporah lived in the Roman period, and if they did so they would have logic on their side.

Horace was of course traumatized by what had happened to him. He'd been captured by large land animals earlier that day, and now saw another prisoner, an innocent bird, a neighbor, slaughtered before his very eyes. And then these monsters collected his neighbor's blood in a basin, and then they turned, their hands still dripping with blood, and came toward Horace. Horace thought to himself: 'This is it. I'll never see my wife and children again. I'll never have a flutter in the hyssop bush with my mistress again.' One of the monsters grabbed him by the neck, dipped him in the blood and swirled him around with a branch of hyssop. Some of the leaves came off and got stuck in poor Horace's feathers. And then he was lifted up and held above the altar. The fierce Middle Eastern sun beat down on him and the blood started to coagulate immediately, glueing the leaves to his feathers. And then he was taken to an open field and let go. Horace was a pyschological wreck, but he managed to fly out of there and cross that field and then another and collapse into his nest, home at last.

His wife, who was named Lucilla, said "Late again, Horace. What's the excuse this time? And you didn't even have the decency to shake the leaves out of your feathers before returning. What is this leaf anyhow? Hyssop. A hyssop leaf. So, your little assignations take place in a hyssop bush, eh? I'll bet I know which one it is, too." Horace said "Lucilla, I am shocked. Shocked at your suspicions. And I want you to know that the ordeal I have just gone through could hardly have been less like your speculation." But Horace was not believed by his wife, or his friends and relations, or even his mistress, who thought he'd gone to some exciting orgy without her. He was shunned by the entire community, and died shortly after, a broken bird.

This incident teaches us that even the most careful ritual of animal sacrifice could, on occasion, lead to injustice.

* See also pages 156-157

¹⁴Thou shalt not curse the deaf, nor put a stumbling-block before the blind, but thou shalt fear thy God: I am the Lord.

The Deaf

Why are we told not to curse those unable to hear properly? Is it only the willfully deaf, who never seem to hear what we say, that are meant? No. It's always important to start with the literal meaning. After all, my friend, those who are deaf can read lips. And watch your hands.

T❧ In the Wilderness

Deuteronomy 3:23-26

²³And I besought the LORD at that time, saying: ²⁴'O Lord GOD, Thou hast begun to show Thy servant Thy greatness, and Thy strong hand; for what god is there in heaven or on earth, that can do according to Thy works, and according to Thy mighty acts? ²⁵Let me go over, I pray Thee, and see the good land that is beyond the Jordan, that goodly hill-country, and Lebanon.' ²⁶But the LORD was wroth with me for your sakes, and hearkened not unto me; and the LORD said unto me: 'Let it suffice thee; speak no more unto Me of this matter.'❧

Let it Suffice

Moses, speaking to the Children of Israel in one of his last exhortations, tells them:

> And I besought the Lord at that time, saying,
> O Lord God ... Let me go over, I pray thee, and
> see the good land that is beyond the Jordan.

God refused Moses' request and warned him:

> Let it suffice thee; speak no more unto Me of this matter.

The anonymous Sages quoted in *Midrash Rabbah* seized on Moses' unsuccessful plea with God to consider the nature of prayer. In the middle of their discussion, the following prayer of Solomon is quoted from I Kings 8:28:

> [H]ave thou respect unto the prayer of thy servant
> and to his supplication, O Lord my God, to hearken unto
> the cry and to the prayer, which thy servant prayeth
> before thee today.

The Sages, noticing Solomon's distinction between "the cry" and "the prayer," comment that "prayer" in this context means praying for one's personal needs. Rabbi Johanan is then quoted as dismissing requests for personal needs with the observation that "no creature has any claim on his Creator." It is whatever Solomon meant by "the cry" that is fundamental to prayer.

A cry can come out of either pleasure or pain, and is the expression of a state so basic that it cannot be properly articulated. As Shakespeare observed in *King Lear* (Act 4, scene 6):

> We came crying hither;
> Thou know'st, the first time that we smell the air
> We waul and cry.

The first whiff of independent existence produces a howl in reaction. But does this cry continue into adulthood? Tennyson, in canto 55 of *In Memoriam*, thought so. He starts with an assertion of vague and uncertain faith and then proceeds to what he knows to be true and real, the cry:

Behold we know not anything:
I can but trust that good shall fall
At last—far off—at last, to all,
And every Winter turn to Spring.

So runs my dream: but what am I?
An infant crying in the night:
An infant crying for the light:
And with no language but a cry.

We cry out for comfort and enlightenment, but to articulate this yearning and need we have, even as adults, no language but a cry.

What are the fundamental cries? I have two candidates, the first from Psalm 22, verse 2:

My God, my God, why have you forsaken me? Why art thou so far from helping me?

In other words, Why do I feel alone in myself?

The second is from Isaiah, chapter 40, verses 6 and 7, in the King James translation:

The voice said, Cry. And he said, What shall I cry? All flesh is grass, and all the goodliness thereof is as the flower of the field: The grass withereth, the flower fadeth: because the spirit of the Lord bloweth upon it: surely the people is grass.

The cry here is "Death!" Why must I die?

But all this concerns only one half of existential cries, the negative cries. What are the fundamental cries of joy? They are, of course, exactly the same. Psalm 22 moves from its opening cry of despair to a cry of affirmation in verse 4, "But Thou art holy." The affirmation in response to "Why have You forsaken me?" is not that help is on its way but that the sense of being alone in ourselves is to be regarded as holy, part of a righteous Creation. This acceptance surely makes sense whether you are a believer or not. It is absurd not to accept the unchangeable, and a mark of sanity to embrace it.

And death? It too is to be praised. As Wallace Stevens put it in his poem, "Sunday Morning"—"Death is the mother of beauty." Without death there would be no poignancy, no true cherishing of moments.

And so, to return to God's response to Moses' plea for his life to be lengthened and his fate altered so that he could go into the promised land:

Let it suffice.

This is one of the great injunctions. In social or political life, of course, it would imply a level of passivity acceptable to almost no one. Like most wisdom it applies to the inner life not the outer life.

Let it suffice. To what does the word 'it' refer? To what is inevitable; at the broadest level, to the fundamental facts of existence, such as death and existential loneliness, that are common to everyone and to which we all have to become reconciled, and if possible embrace, in our own way.

Deuteronomy 4:25-28

²⁵When thou shalt beget children, and children's children, and ye shall have been long in the land, and shall deal corruptly, and make a graven image, even the form of any living thing, and shall do that which is evil in the sight of the LORD thy God, to provoke Him; ²⁶I call heaven and earth to witness against you this day, that ye shall utterly perish from off the land whereunto ye go over the Jordan to possess it; ye shall not prolong your days upon it, but shall utterly be destroyed. ²⁷And the LORD shall scatter you among the peoples, and ye shall be left few in number among the nations, whither the LORD shall lead you away. ²⁸And there ye shall serve gods, the work of men's hands, wood and stone, which neither see, nor hear, nor eat, nor smell.➔

Wood and Stone

. . . gods, the work of men's hands,
wood and stone.

[Deuteronomy 4.28]

Perhaps not idols. Relics. I've a shirt
she mended. The stitching still is fine and strong
but if I wear it it will wear away.
An old green zippered sewing kit she used.
Even some strands of hair culled from her comb.
Photos, of course, the ones she kept on her
dressing table, and the set she had
inside her bag. A scarf or two. And her
piece of opalescent Roman glass—
did it have that shimmer when it was in use?
And letters. She used to add a bit each day.
And a necklace, an Egyptian amulet.
I knew she'd look it up so I made sure
it was no god of death I'd given her.

Deuteronomy 8:2

²And thou shalt remember all the way which the LORD thy God
hath led thee these forty years in the wilderness, to humble thee, and
to prove thee, to know what was in thine heart, whether thou wouldest
keep his commandments, or no. ❧

Translation: King James Version

Approaching Fifty
[Deuteronomy 8:2]

And you shall remember all the way

one or two early intimations:
turning back (at four, on a family picnic)
to examine a single pink wildflower,
and then running to catch up with the others;
stooping (at seven, a beach in Queensland)
to scrutinize an unusual shell and be
shocked when I noticed it was broken.

These forty years in the wilderness

And then, after her death, sorting through
a drawer in her dressing table, I recognized
a coloured scarf I'd given my mother
had touched her.
                    To humble you, to test you,
to know what was in your heart.

U✍ Kings and Prophets

2 Samuel 6:14-16

¹⁴And David danced before the LORD with all his might; and David was girded with a linen ephod. ¹⁵So David and all the house of Israel brought up the ark of the LORD with shouting, and with the sound of the horn.

¹⁶And it was so, as the ark of the LORD came into the city of David, that Michal the daughter of Saul looked out at the window, and saw King David leaping and dancing before the LORD; and she despised him in her heart.✍

David

Donatello's David has its elegance,
a slender polished body, long straight hair,
a spare rock in one cocky hand on hip.
And yet Goliath's sword is awkward, it's
too heavy for this kid; he looks to me
a bit off balance; he's leaning on that sword.
Well, after all, he had just killed a man.
I'm not ungrateful but I would prefer

a David who is wise, a Chinese sage
reclining in 'the position of royal ease,'

or an Egyptian David, upright, with both feet
placed firmly on the ground in stable stride,

or David as perfected being who
offers a calming gesture with his hand,

or, if I have to live with what I've got,
a David *leaping and dancing* like a fool.

1 Kings 3:5-10

⁵At Gibeon the LORD appeared to Solomon in a dream by night; and God said, "Ask, what shall I grant you?" ⁶Solomon said, "You dealt most graciously with Your servant my father David, because he walked before You in faithfulness and righteousness and in integrity of heart. You have continued this great kindness to him by giving him a son to occupy his throne, as is now the case. ⁷And now, O LORD my God, You have made Your servant king in place of my father David; but I am a young lad, *-with no experience in leadership-*. ⁸Your servant finds himself in the midst of the people You have chosen, a people too numerous to be numbered or counted. ⁹Grant then, Your servant an understanding mind to judge Your people, to distinguish between good and bad; for who can judge this vast people of Yours?"

¹⁰The LORD was pleased that Solomon had asked for this.➥

Translation: JPS 1985

- Lit. "I do not know to go out and come in"; cf. Num.27:17

Ask

God said to Solomon, "Ask, what shall I grant you?" Solomon wanted "an understanding mind." What requisite would I request? Something permitting me to detect the hidden sources I seek. A divining rod.

Isaiah 3:18-23 and 4:4

[18]In that day the LORD will take away the finery of the anklets, the headbands, and the crescents; [19]the pendants, the bracelets, and the scarfs; [20]the headdresses, the armlets, the sashes, the perfume boxes, and the amulets; [21]the signet rings and nose rings; [22]the festal robes, the mantles, the cloaks, and the handbags; [23]the garments of gauze, the linen garments, the turbans, and the veils.

. . .

[4]when the LORD will have washed away the filth of the daughters of Zion and cleansed the bloodstains of Jerusalem from its midst by a spirit of judgment and by a spirit of burning.

Translation: Revised Standard Version

Rouge

Like Isaiah I was disgusted by
pendant gems, silk, frills, by
the garments of gauze, the linen garments,
and repulsed by made-up flesh, by creams,
mascara, shadow, rouge, by the desire
to mask part of oneself, the breathing
skin, with a cover of dead substance,
by the kiss of lips smeared with pigment.

And yet in this phase of purity it was
a diamond's gleam of random light
sparkling at sudden angles as she moved
and a streak of rouge along her hidden bone
that allured me by brightness to
what was there, *that washed away the filth.*

Isaiah 35:5-7

[5]Then the eyes of the blind shall be opened,
And the ears of the deaf shall be unstopped.
[6]Then shall the lame man leap as a hart,
And the tongue of the dumb shall sing;
For in the wilderness shall waters break out,
And streams in the desert.
[7]And the parched land shall become a pool,
And the thirsty ground springs of water;
In the habitation of jackals herds shall lie down,
It shall be an enclosure for reeds and rushes. ❧

Home
[Australia]

The centre of the land in which I came to life
is unremitting red desert stretching
its monotonous prospect to thin horizons,
an aridity as immense as some other lands.

And yet when rains come they come in torrents
creating rivers which pour into vast depressions,
lapsed lakes waiting for replenishment
to return to them their name and purpose.

And then the desert displays what was dormant within it,
the grass seed preserved throughout parched seasons,
and yields a springtime that even has flowers
until heat evaporates the reaches of water

and once more rivers and lakes dry out to depression
and loam desiccates to hard clay
and winds traverse that unperturbed surface,
the heart of the land in which I came to life.

Jeremiah 8:21-22

[21]For the hurt of the daughter of my people
    am I seized with anguish;
I am black, appalment hath taken hold on me.
[22]Is there no balm in Gilead?
Is there no physician there?
Why then is not the health
Of the daughter of my people recovered?◐

Balm in Gilead

"Is there no balm in Gilead?" asks Jeremiah rhetorically in an aside that has attracted no learned commentary. Is this, perhaps, a sentence that could have been omitted from Holy Scripture? But, if it had been omitted, then slaves, living two and a half thousand years later, and on the other side of an ocean unknown to Jeremiah, would have been deprived of their great song.

V🐢 Psalms

Psalm 1

Blessed is the man
who walks not in the counsel of the wicked,
nor stands in the way of sinners,
   nor sits in the seat of scoffers;
²but his delight is in the law of the LORD,
   and on his law he meditates day and night.
³He is like a tree
   planted by streams of water,
that yields its fruit in its season,
   and its leaf does not wither.
In all that he does, he prospers.

⁴The wicked are not so,
   but are like chaff which the wind drives away.
⁵Therefore the wicked will not stand in the judgment,
   nor sinners in the congregation of the righteous;
⁶for the LORD knows the way of the righteous,
   but the way of the wicked will perish.

Translation: Revised Standard Version

Psalm 1

Blessed is the man not born
in Lodz in the wrong decade,
who walks not in tree-lined shade
like my father's father in this photo, *nor*
stands in the way of sinners waiting for
his yellow star,
nor sits, if he could sit, in their cattle car,

but his delight is being born
as I was, in Australia, far away
and on God's law he meditates night and day.

He is like a tree that's granted
the land where it is planted,
that yields its fruit by reason
of sun and rain in season.

The wicked are not so, they
burn their uniforms and walk away.

Therefore the wicked are like Cain
who offered fruit which God chose to disdain

and the way of the righteous is Abel's, whose
sacrifice God chose to choose
and who was murdered anyway.

Psalm 8:3-5

[3]When I consider thy heavens, the work of thy fingers,
the moon and the stars, which thou hast ordained;
[4]What is man, that thou art mindful of him? and the son
of man, that thou visitest him?
[5]For thou hast made him a little lower than the angels,
and hast crowned him with glory and honour. ❧

Translation: King James Version

The Work
[Psalm 8]

When I consider thy heavens, the work of thy fingers,
I recall an unshaven Yugoslav shoemaker
my mother took me to when I was ten
who carved my foot's last in wood,
and remember the edge of his cut leather,
the clean line behind the knife,
and his thick stitches binding, for a childish
ingrate, the crafted object to be worn away.

Thou hast crowned him with glory and honor.
And yesterday I came across a photo
from a lost campaign in a poor country:
a bandit has pulled off his hat
and stands at attention against a wall,
not defiant, not contrite, merely dignified.

Psalm 8:10

[10]O Lord, our Lord,
How glorious is Thy name in all the earth!◆

To King David

I know, my namesake, you didn't write
all the psalms, and certainly not those howls
from out of Babylon, the first exile
where remnants of your nation, stunned,
adjusted after the first destruction.
And yet these Praises—the collection's name—
and petitions, arguments, and more straightforward
cries, are rightly (so I feel) ascribed to you
since, it turns out, in spite of your adulteries
and orders to murder loyal colleagues, friends,
you were—your reign and Solomon's—our people's
brief glory.
           Yet I and other poets don't
envy you for that, not even for
the life which wrung composition out of you,
but for the settings in temples, synagogues,
catacombs, monasteries, cathedrals, hospices,
in which your Praises have been chanted, sung,
recited, read, whispered, remembered, in
the night before a battle, near sick beds,
in prisons, slave plantations, gulags, the death camps;
and for the Psalters—painted, printed—where
your Hebrew words were scripted into patterns of
Greek, Latin, Amharic, Cyrillic, Devanagari;
and for the timbrels, pipes, cymbals, strings,
named in the short last psalm that someone made,
some lucky poet, who might have heard it chanted as
priests walked up the Temple steps to where
they'd splash the sacrificial blood and still,
three thousand years beyond those Bronze Age rites,
it still is chanted by the remnants who now live
in Melbourne, Buenos Aires, New York, Prague,
who also sing a simple line of yours which says
How glorious is Your name in all the earth.

Psalm 102:5-8

[5]Because of my loud groaning
    my bones cleave to my flesh.
[6]I am like a vulture* of the wilderness,
    like an owl of the waste places;
[7]I lie awake,
    I am like a lonely bird on the housetop.
[8]All the day my enemies taunt me,
    those that deride me use my name for a curse.

Translation: Revised Standard Version

* The meaning of the Hebrew word is uncertain.

The Owl: A Dream
[Psalm 102]

There was commotion, pointing to a roof.
An owl was perched and looking at the grass
then plunged to what she saw; her claws went out
and she retrieved a piece of paper with

the photo of a mouse. We were amused.
And later on the people who'd been there
were in the barroom when the owl came in.
She asked me: "Was it funny when I caught

something inanimate?" But I kept quiet.
The others sidled out. We were alone,
conversing, when she quoted from the psalm:

"Like an owl of the waste places I lie awake,
a lonely bird on the housetop; all the day
my enemies taunt me." It seemed to comfort her.

Psalm 119:1-9

Blessed are those whose way is blameless,
   who walk in the law of the LORD!
²Blessed are those who keep his testimonies,
   who seek him with their whole heart,
³who also do not wrong,
   but walk in his ways!
⁴Thou hast commanded thy precepts
   to be kept diligently.
⁵O that my ways may be steadfast
   in keeping thy statutes!
⁶Then shall I not be put to shame,
   having my eyes fixed on all thy commandments.
⁷I will praise thee with an upright heart,
   when I learn thy righteous ordinances.
⁸I will observe thy statutes;
   O forsake me not utterly!
⁹How can a young man keep his way pure?
   By guarding it according to thy word.

Translation: Revised Standard Version

The Blameless
[Psalm 119]

Blessed are those whose way is blameless. But
do they exist? The evidence is bleak.
Adam and Eve of course, don't fit the bill;
and the first murderer's no good, although
he got protection; Abel didn't last—
to have a blameless life you have to live—
and Noah, "righteous in his generation," was,
the rabbis tell us, righteous only when
compared with those God wiped out in the Flood;
and Abraham talked back, and tried to kill his son,
and threw a helpless woman and her child
into the desert with one loaf of bread,
and served non-kosher when God came to lunch;
and Sarah laughed at God and beat the servants; Lot
committed incest at least twice while drunk;
and passive Isaac much preferred the son
God didn't want; and Jacob, as we know,
stole, although his inability
to bargain when in love redeems him in my eyes;
and Joseph as a child was an obnoxious brat
and later was a prig and, when he had the chance,
tortured his father over Benjamin;
and Moses was a murderer in his youth,
which could perhaps be justified, but still
he had a temper, smashed the stones on which
God had engraved commandments for us all,
and, after, ordered a general massacre.
Should I go on? Joshua's atrocities
have turned much stronger stomachs than my own.
And David? He's no prig, for sure, and who am I
to hold adultery against him, but
to send the husband to the front and have him killed
was, I must be frank with you, not nice.

I come back to the psalm, which asks (verse nine)
How can a young man keep his way pure?

And the ladies have their problems too, I know.

Psalm 137:1-2

By the rivers of Babylon,
There we sat down, yea, we wept,
When we remembered Zion.
²Upon the willows in the midst thereof
We hanged up our harps.❧

The Gardens

Melbourne's Botanic Gardens! where I came
to walk along the bordered paths with him,
and pose in short pants for the photos placed
into this album I'm now leafing through,
and eat my sandwiches beside the lake,
and cast bread on the water for the swans.
And later, when we met on Sundays, we
went off to European movies, then
to his small room where we played chess. He cut
his dense black bread held close up to his chest.
One afternoon we passed the synagogue
and saw some litter scattered on its steps
including lobster shells. He said "This is
deliberate desecration. They must know
lobster isn't kosher." "Daddy, it's not that,
it's an Australian picnic. Not cleaned up."
I thought it was absurd he didn't know.

This must have been round nineteen fifty-five.
A mere ten years had passed. And in four years
he'd suicide, and I would read the documents
he kept inside their envelopes in a wood box—
certificates of immigration, change
of name, degrees, but mainly photographs
and letters from his parents and his friends.
And then I found a letter he had sent
to Poland. The final one. It said, "I wish
I could protect you from the sadists," and was stamped
"Unable to deliver." Somehow I
was not aware. He never talked of it.
And now I try to visualize what happened to
his parents and those smiling friends of his,
and try to understand how it would feel
orphaned, divorced, recalling, to walk in
the gardens of Babylon, and not weep.

Antiphons

Psalm 32:1

Blessed is the man in whose spirit there is no guile.
And of the crafty, those who are plain in style.

*

Psalm 16:9

My flesh shall rest in hope.
Not if it's given too much scope.

Psalm 17:15

I shall be satisfied when I awake
but as the day wears on my head begins to ache.

Psalm 22:1

My God, my God, why hast thou forsaken me?
Who knows? In any case, He's let you be.

Psalm 22:26

They shall praise the LORD who seek him.
But, like Moses, you're in danger if you meet him.

Psalm 23:6

Surely goodness and mercy shall follow me.
But will they overtake? Well, we'll see.

Psalm 31:5

Into thy hand I commit my spirit: thou
can have it. But the body's mine for now.

Psalm 31:10

For my life is spent with grief, and my years with sighing
from which I've wrung a laugh or two, and skill at lying.

Psalm 38:6

I go mourning all day long.
For God's sake sing; there's plenty of sad song.

Psalm 39:4

LORD, *make me to know mine end.*
Sure. Cross my palm with silver, friend.

Psalm 102:1

Hear my prayer, O LORD, and let my cry
be ignored. My prayer? Let me give up my cry.

*

Psalm 25:7

Remember not the sins of my youth, nor my
youthful good deeds. But hear this adult sigh.

Annotations to the Psalms
for Sarah

Psalm 39:12

I am a stranger, as all my fathers were.
As Abraham was, even when still in Ur.

*

Psalm 8:2

Out of the mouths of babes and sucklings thou hast ordained
howls and gurgles, by which their world's explained.

Psalm 18:19

He brought me forth also into a large place
consisting of both inner and outer space.

Psalm 18:20

The LORD rewarded me according to the cleanness of
my hands. And there are stains you can't remove.

Psalm 22:14

I am poured out like water into some
receptacle, which gives the shape to come.

Psalm 37:4

He shall give thee the desires of thine heart.
 And then you'll know the desires with which to part.

Psalm 38:18

I will be sorry for my sin.
But for now the pleasure takes me in.

Psalm 104:25

Things creeping innumerable both small and great
live energetically, accepting fate.

Psalm 106:20

They changed their glory into the similitude of an ox,
which was, of course, at the time, more orthodox.

Psalm 106:24

Yea, they despised the pleasant land, they believed
they could subdue the earth. They were deceived.

Psalm 102:9

For I have mingled my drink with weeping
and diluted with drink the life in my keeping.

Psalm 102:11

My days are like a shadow that declineth.
Life seems less dark as I approach my death.

Psalm 102:25

The heavens are the work of thy hands.
But light and life required commands.

*

Psalm 11:1

How say ye to my soul, Flee as a bird
to your mountain?
            Sarah, if anything is, this is the Word.

W⟍ Proverbs

Proverbs 3:1-3

My son, forget not my teaching;
   But let thy heart keep my commandments;
²For length of days, and years of life,
   And peace, will they add to thee.
³Let not kindness and truth forsake thee;
   Bind them about thy neck,
      Write them upon the table of thy heart[.]⟍

Forget Not
[Proverbs 3:1]

My son, forget not my teaching—recall

our conversation on the word "sadism," when I
maintained the main medical definition
was pain inflicted while making love
and how you insisted (as if important
to you at fourteen!) the meaning was broader;
and recall my advice to forego your affection
for physics and become a physician so that
if you failed at research you could have a recourse;
and recall that I never remarried and lived alone,
and recall your visits to my sparse rented
furnished rooms, our common silence
filled in with games of chess, and recall
coming into the kitchen in your mother's house
to be told I was dead and how it happened
and the hours over years of meditation on
your part in the silence that led to suicide— ·

and let your heart keep my commandments.

Proverbs 6:6-8

[6]Go to the ant, thou sluggard;
   Consider her ways, and be wise;
[7]Which having no chief,
   Overseer, or ruler,
[8]Provideth her bread in the summer,
   And gatherest her food in the harvest.❧

The Ant
Proverbs 6:6

Go to the ant, thou sluggard,

and watch it lug an object
forward single file
with no short breaks for
coffee, gossip, a croissant,

and no stopping to apostrophize
blossom, by-passed because
pollen is not its job,
no pause for trampled companions:

consider her ways—and be content.

Proverbs 15:23

²³A man hath joy in the answer of his mouth;
And a word in due season, how good is it!☙

The Answer
for Michèle

Winter, Fifth Avenue. Half a block south
of Central Park. It blurted out. Ten years ago.
"You're as lovely as the falling snow."

A man hath joy in the answer of his mouth

And you were startled by what you understood.

And, spoken in their moment, words are good.

Proverbs 17:1

Better is a dry morsel with quiet
than a house full of feasting with strife.

Translation: Revised Standard Version

A Dry Morsel
[Proverbs 17:1]

Better is a dry morsel with quiet

and a key turning in a front lock,
and a door that opens on empty rooms,
and a lonely mouth watering at the thought
of a kiss as it reads a trashy romance,
and a death undiscovered for several days,
and a funeral to which few come,

than a house full of feasting with strife.

X ❧ The Book of Job

Job 1:8-12

⁸And the Lᴏʀᴅ said unto Satan: 'Hast thou considered My servant Job, that there is none like him in the earth, a whole-hearted and an upright man, one that feareth God, and shunneth evil?' ⁹Then Satan answered the Lᴏʀᴅ, and said: 'Doth Job fear God for nought? ¹⁰Hast not Thou made a hedge about him, and about his house, and about all that he hath, on every side? Thou hast blessed the work of his hands, and his possessions are increased in the land. ¹¹But put forth Thy hand now, and touch all that he hath, surely he will blaspheme Thee to Thy face.' ¹²And the Lᴏʀᴅ said unto Satan: 'Behold, all that he hath is in thy power; only upon himself put not forth thy hand.' So Satan went forth from the presence of the Lᴏʀᴅ. ❧

Omniscience

It was curiosity that prompted God to let Satan experiment on Job and his family. After all, God's omniscience has its limits. A truly free choice can't be foreseen, although God's guesses are usually accurate. But people in comfortable circumstances, who have kept themselves clean, who have never failed, who seem to have no faults, are always a puzzle, to themselves as well as God.

Job 1:18-22

[18]While he was yet speaking, there came also another, and said: 'Thy sons and thy daughters were eating and drinking wine in their eldest brother's house; [19]and, behold, there came a great wind from across the wilderness, and smote the four corners of the house, and it fell upon the young people, and they are dead; and I only am escaped to tell thee.'

[20]Then Job arose, and rent his mantle, and shaved his head, and fell down upon the ground, and worshipped; [21]and he said:

> Naked came I out of my mother's womb,
> And naked shall I return thither;
> The LORD gave and the LORD hath taken away;
> Blessed be the name of the LORD.

[22]For all this Job sinned not, nor ascribed aught unseemly to God.

Moral Knowledge

Satan's experiment to find out Job's true character involved killing Job's children. Moral knowledge, it seems, is never costless. And the cost of moral knowledge in one person is usually—perhaps always—borne by many, some innocent. As a character says in Doris Lessing's novel, *The Golden Notebook* (Bantam, 1981, page 626):

> Every bloody one of them's got a history of emotional crime, oh the sad bleeding corpses that litter the road to maturity of the wise serene man or woman of fifty-odd!

I read this when I was in my twenties and put a little pencil mark in the margin since it seemed worth remembering.

And now I'm over fifty myself.

Job 2:3-9, 13 and 3:1-3

[3]And the LORD said to Satan: "Have you considered my servant
Job, that there is none like him on the earth, a blameless and upright
man, who fears God, and turns away from evil? He still holds fast to
his integrity, although you moved me against him, to destroy him
without cause." [4]Then Satan answered the LORD, "Skin for skin! All that
a man has he will give for his life. [5]But put forth thy hand now, and
touch his bone and his flesh, and he will curse thee to thy face." [6]And
the LORD said to Satan: "Behold, he is in your power; only spare his
life."

[7]So Satan went forth from the presence of the LORD, and afflicted
Job with loathsome sores from the sole of his foot to the crown of his
head. [8]And he took a potsherd with which to scrape himself, and he sat
among the ashes. [9]Then said his wife to him: "Do you still hold fast to
your integrity? Curse God, and die."

. . .

[13]And they sat with him on the ground seven days and seven
nights, and no one spoke a word to him, for they saw that his suffering
was very great.

. . .

3[1]After this Job opened his mouth, and cursed the day of his
birth. [2]And Job said:

> [3]"Let the day perish wherein I was born,
> and the night which said,
> 'A man-child is conceived.'
> [4]Let that day be darkness!
> May God above not seek it,
> nor light shine upon it.
> [5]Let gloom and deep darkness claim it.
> Let clouds dwell upon it;
> let the blackness of the day terrify it . . ."

Translation: Revised Standard Version

The Problem of Evil

Job's wife advised him to "Curse God and die." Given what we know and she didn't, this seems an approach to the problem of evil, if we insist on worrying about it, as justified as any.

Job, the pious victim, pined for death only when he himself was affected. He could bear to live after the destruction of his loved ones, as indeed is the case with most survivors.

Job 4:1 and 4:12-17

Then Eliphaz the Temanite, answered and said,

. . .

¹²Now a thing was secretly brought to me, and mine
ear received a little thereof.
¹³In thoughts from the visions of the night, when deep sleep
falleth on men,
¹⁴Fear came upon me, and trembling, which made all my
bones to shake.
¹⁵Then a spirit passed before my face; the hair of my flesh
stood up;
¹⁶It stood still, but I could not discern the form thereof:
an image was before mine eyes, there was silence, and I
heard a voice, saying,
¹⁷Shall mortal man be more just than God? shall a man be
more pure than his Maker?

Translation: King James Version

Hearing

Job's friends sat with him and shared his grief in silence for seven days, and then they attempted to comprehend. The very first friend, Eliphaz the Temanite, recalled a dream in which he heard a voice asking rhetorically whether "mortal man" was more just than God. This line of argument is the same as that directed at Job by the Voice Out of the Whirlwind. But Job dismissed Eliphaz and was convinced by the Whirlwind. So, whom you hear things from does matter, and this is one of the many lessons taught by the Book of Job.

Job 42:7-10

⁷And it was so, that after the Lord had spoken these words unto Job, the Lord said to Eliphaz the Temanite: 'My wrath is kindled against thee, and against thy two friends; for ye have not spoken of Me the thing that is right, as My servant Job hath. ⁸Now therefore, take unto you seven bullocks and seven rams, and go to My servant Job, and offer up for yourselves a burnt-offering; and My servant Job shall pray for you; for him will I accept, that I do not unto you aught unseemly; for ye have not spoken of Me the thing that is right, as My servant Job hath.' ⁹So Eliphaz the Temanite and Bildad the Shuhite and Zophar the Naamathite went, and did according as the Lord commanded them; and the Lord accepted Job. ¹⁰And the Lord changed the fortune of Job, when he prayed for his friends; and the Lord gave Job twice as much as he had before.

Understanding

Job, who howled and didn't listen to his friends' honest efforts at understanding, is amply rewarded. His friends are punished for wrong reasoning. Satan, whose hypothesis was, after all, sound, is ignored.

Creatures who try to understand everything irritate the Master of the Universe.

Y. The Talmud

Tractate Abodah Zarah 2b.

[I]n commenting on the verse: "And they stood at the nether part of the mountain"* R. Dimi b. Hama said, "This teaches us that the Holy One, blessed be He, suspended the mountain over Israel like a vault† and said to them, 'If you accept the Torah, it will go well with you, but if not this place will be your grave.'"

Translation: Soncino Talmud

---

* Exodus 19:17
† Lit. "cask" or "tub"

The Talmud on Free Will

When Moses brought the people from their camp
toward Mount Sinai, where they'd meet with God,
they stood (I quote) "at the nether part of the mount."
But why this strange locution, "nether part"?
It is, says Rabbi Dimi (the son of Hama,
the Babylonian sage), to teach us that
the Holy One lifted the mountain up
(like a huge tub) and held it over them
so all were under the vastness of its base
which blotted out the sun and was, when they
looked up, the only thing they saw. And then,
silenced in its shadow, they all shook
with the reverberations of the Voice,
which, we are told, even the deaf could hear,
when God opened his mouth and spoke these words:
"If you accept my Law, then well and good,
if not I'll crush you with this." They agreed.

Line 14: We are told "even the deaf could hear" in *Pesikta de-Rab Kahana*, 12:19 (New Haven: Yale University Press, 1975), page 198.

Pirke Avot 2

Rabbi Simeon says:

> Be meticulous about the recitation of the *Shema*
> and the *Prayer*.
>
> And when you pray don't treat your praying as a matter of
> routine; but let it be a [plea for] mercy and
> supplication before the Omnipresent, the blessed, as it
> is said, *For He is gracious and full of*
> *compassion, slow to anger and full of mercy, and*
> *repents of the evil.*
>
> And never be evil in your own eyes.

Translation by Jacob Neusner.

In Your Own Eyes
Pirke Avot 2

Rabbi Simeon said: "Never be evil in your own eyes." A hard rule, rabbi!

Late one afternoon when I was six or so, my mother sent me off to bed as punishment. Almost fifty years later I can still recall the moment I continued to cry when I could have stopped, the moment of choice after which my sobs were false, and the sense of triumph when she came at last to comfort me. My first small revenge, and the knowledge that went with it.

Pirke Avot 2

Rabbi Eleazar says:
Be constant in learning of Torah;
And know what to reply to an Epicurean;
And know before whom you work, for your employer can be
depended upon to pay your wages for what you do. ✍

Translation by Jacob Neusner.

Rabbi Eleazar

for Lori Seibel

I

Rabbi Eleazar said: "Know what to reply
to an Epicurean." But what if she winks her eye?

Rabbi, across two thousand years I feel
your irritation at my smart-arsed rhyme
and grant your question jabs at all of us
· relishers who find sex, food, work, art,
and even love is not enough, and don't know why.

II

And yet your Talmud colleague, Rav, remarked
that after death each person must account
"for every thing his eye saw that he didn't eat,"
a comment now interpreted to mean
all permitted pleasures he could have had
but didn't, as his life was eaten up
here, where it is possible to fondle everything.

And so, for you, too, Eleazar, I suppose
there must have been some problems in all this.

Lines 8-10: The Jerusalem Talmud, Tractate Kiddushin (Marriage), 4:12, 66d.

Z. The Midrash

Genesis Rabbah LXI.1

It is written, *Happy is the man that hath not walked in the counsel of the wicked* (Ps. 1:1). *"Happy is the man"* refers to Abraham[.]

Translation: *Midrash Rabbah*, The Soncino Press, 1983.

The Psalm of Abraham*
Prooftexts from the Koran

Happy is the man: This is Abraham, as it is said in the Koran, Sura 4, "And God took Abraham for a friend."

that hath not walked in the counsel of the wicked, as it is said in the Koran, Sura 21, with God speaking in the royal plural, "We gave Abraham his rectitude."

He shall be like a tree . . . that brings forth fruit in its season, as it is said in the Koran, Sura 2, "Abraham said, 'My Lord, make this land secure and provide its people with fruits.'"

and in whatever he does he shall prosper, as it is said in the Koran, Sura 21, referring to the midrashic story of Abraham being cast into the fiery furnace by Nimrod, "We said, 'O fire, be coolness and safety for Abraham.'"

For the Lord regards the way of the righteous, as it is said in the Koran, Sura 11, "Our messengers came to Abraham with good tidings; they said, "Peace!""

but the way of the wicked shall perish, as it is said in the Koran, Sura 108, "Surely those who hate are the ones cut off."

*See page 114 for the full text of Psalm 1.

Leviticus Rabbah XVI.2*

THIS SHALL BE THE LAW OF THE LEPER, etc. (Leviticus 14:1) This is alluded to in what is written, "Who is the man that desireth life?" (Psalm 34:13) ... What is written [immediately] thereafter?— "Keep thy tongue from evil, depart from evil and do good." R. Jannai said: Solomon, too, proclaims, "Whoso keepeth his mouth and his tongue keepeth his soul from troubles" (Proverbs 21:23). R. Jannai said ... It is for the same reason that Moses addressed a warning to Israel, saying to them THIS SHALL BE THE LAW OF THE *METZORA* (LEPER), i.e. the law relating to one that gives currency to an evil report *(motzi [shem] ra).*

Translation: *Midrash Rabbah*, 3d ed., Soncino Press 1983.

---

* The passage depends on a pun on the Hebrew word *metzora*, which means, or at least is conventionally translated as, "leper." The rabbis of the Midrash, who loved puns, read *metzora* as *motzi ra*, meaning "brings forth evil," or *motzi [shem] ra*, meaning "brings forth [the name of] evil," which they understood, for the purposes of their exposition, as a reference to slander and gossip. In the midrash opposite I have imitated this by giving a contemporary exposition of the same biblical text that depends on and leads up to a pun on the English word "leper." See page 93 for another midrash on the same passage from Leviticus.

The Leaper*

Our text is Leviticus 14:2, "This shall be the law of the leper in the day of his cleansing: he shall be brought unto a priest." The Israelite ritual of cleansing a leper consisted of bringing the leper to a priest on the day of his cleansing, and having the priest examine him to see if the signs of the disease were gone. If so, the priest was to conduct a ritual in which one bird is killed and another bird dipped into its blood, along with a small branch of hyssop—an aromatic shrub—and then taken to an open field and let go. The leper is sprinkled with the blood on the hyssop branch.

How are we to understand this Bronze Age ritual in contemporary terms? We must understand the social function it fullfilled. And to do this best we should try to think of a functional equivalent in our own society, preferably one we have participated in. The ritual of cleansing the leper is nothing other than a graduation or, if you prefer, a commencement ceremony. Our graduation ritual occurs after the student has been brought to the functional equivalent of a priest, and been examined. But even when this examination reveals that the disease of ignorance—of engineering, or medicine or law or the Talmud—has been cured, the student is not yet free to go out into society and practice a profession. There must be a social certification process without which the student, even though objectively qualified, cannot be accepted into a community of practitioners. The ritual of cleansing or graduating marks a change in social status, from the status of being unclean, a leper, a student, to the status of being clean, cured, a graduate. The ritual marks a change from a lower to a higher status, a quantum leap in status.

And that, of course, is why Leviticus 14:2 can be read:

This shall be the law of the *leaper* in the day of his cleansing.

* See also pages 92 and 93

Bet haMidrash 1:153-154

. . .

[T]he Holy One, blessed be He, beckons the angel in charge of the souls and says to him: "Bring me that particular soul!" For this is how it is done when they are created from the day the world was created until the world comes to an end. Immediately the soul comes before the Holy One, blessed be He, and prostrates itself before Him. In that hour the Holy One, blessed be He, says to it: "Enter into this drop!" But the soul opens up its mouth and says to Him: "Master of the World! I am satisfied with the world I have been in from the day in which I was created. If it please You, do not make me enter this evil-smelling drop, for I am holy and pure." The Holy One, blessed be He, says to it: "The world which I make you enter is better than the world in which you have been, and when I created you I did not do so except for this drop." Then the Holy One, blessed be He, places it against its will into that drop, and the angel comes and puts the soul into the bowels of its mother

. . .

And the embryo lies in the bowels of his mother nine months.

. . .

And when his time comes to emerge into the world, he argues: "Did I not already say before Him who spoke and caused the world to be that I am satisfied with the world in which I have been dwelling." And He says to him: "The world which I make you enter is good. Morever, against your will are you formed in the bowels of your mother, and against your will are you born and do you emerge into the world!"

. . . ➥

Translated from the Hebrew by Raphael Patai.

An Old Story
from the Bet haMidrash

It is said:

In Heaven at the hour before conception
the Holy One commands a chosen soul,
"Enter that ovum!" But the soul protests,
"I'm pure and satisfied, don't push me to
pollute myself for that disgusting drop."
Then the Master of the Universe says, "Soul!
the filth you must join up with is
good, you were created to be there"

and places it inside against its will.
And after the gestation time is over
the soul again argues it is content
and again God says to it, "The world
is good, and not the womb you're in, and you,
against your will, crying, must emerge."

Index of Titles